CAN A BRIDGE BUILD ITSELF?

Essays on Belief and Moral Values

CAN A BRIDGE BUILD ITSELF?

Essays on Belief and Moral Values

Edited by
Omer A. Ergi

New Jersey

Copyright © 2025 by Tughra Books

First published in 2012

28 27 26 25   4 5 6 7

All rights reserved. No part of this book may be reproduced or transmitted in any form or by any means, electronic or mechanical, including photocopying, recording or by any information storage and retrieval system without permission in writing from the Publisher.

Published by Tughra Books
335 Clifton Avenue
Clifton, New Jersey 07011

www.tughrabooks.com

Library of Congress Cataloging-in-Publication Data Available

ISBN: 978-1-59784-297-6

Printed in Canada

Contents

Introduction ix
   On reading ix

CHAPTER ONE

1. Signs in the window 1
2. Can a bridge build itself? 2
3. Various evidences regarding the existence of Allah 5
4. Is it possible that matter came into existence by chance? 6
5. Rights of a mother and father 7
6. A mother's heart 8
7. Compassion of mothers 8
8. Manners 9
9. Respecting our teachers 10
10. How did they correct a wrong? 11

CHAPTER TWO

1. A cell will tell 13
2. The unity whispered by the animals 14
3. Examples from humans 16
4. Everything points to God 17
5. Why cannot we see God? 17
6. Status of belief 18
7. Essence of friendship 19
8. It is difficult to repair a broken heart 20
9. Trust 21
10. Humanity 21
11. Being human 23
12. To become a refined human being 24
13. Morals 25

CHAPTER THREE

1. Arguments against faith 27
2. Universal harmony 30
3. Delicate balance in nature 31
4. Everything indicates to Him 32
5. If God created everything, then who created God? 34
6. How can we believe in things that we cannot see? 36
7. The tree of faith 37
8. Faith of a handicapped child 38
9. Taking advice 39
10. Benefiting from Divine Mercy 40
11. The owner of the word 41

CHAPTER FOUR

1. Young person 43
2. Tito's historical confessions 43
3. Sir Isaac Newton 45
4. Evidence of God's existence 47
5. A million proofs 47
6. A blind man 48
7. Lying 49

CHAPTER FIVE

First word 53
Second word 55
   1. Thoughts on vehicles 58
   2. Those that brightened the middle ages 59
   3. Return to life 63

CHAPTER SIX

Third word 67
   1. A prescription for happiness 69
   2. Noble Messenger encourages Muslims to pray 73
   3. A head that does not perform bow before Allah 75
   4. Worship 76
   5. Brake failure 77

CHAPTER SEVEN

Fourth word 81
   1. Salah and Swedish gymnastics 83
   2. Sacrifice 84
   3. The green suit 87
   4. The Salah that takes you to Paradise 88
   5. Salah wipes out sins 88
   6. Salah 89
   7. Young man, have you ever thought about this? ... 93
   8. He did not miss his prayer 94
   9. Salah in the words of the noble Prophet 94

CHAPTER EIGHT

1. Youth 101
2. Obsessive feelings and light at the peak 102
3. The incredible efficiency of the human body 107
4. Warnings and admonitions 110
5. How did Ali perform his prayers? 113
6. The man who became imam to the angels 113

CHAPTER NINE

Twenty-first word first station 115
   1. Reflections on salah 121
   2. Rewards of tahajjud 130
   3. Who is a Prophet? 131
   4. A humanity in the absence of Prophets 133
   5. Prophethood 135
   7. Did you know? 137

CHAPTER TEN

Nineteenth word 141
   1. The last pearl in the crown of Prophethood 146
   2. Precious hair 149
   3. History and time testifies to his Prophethood 151
   4. The pride of humanity 151
   5. Body in the hands of spirituality 153
   6. Lost letter 156

CHAPTER ELEVEN

1. Miracles of the Messenger of Allah 159
2. Why did the man who ate halva, have himself stoned? 169
3. Servanthood 170
4. The pride of humanity 172

CHAPTER TWELVE

1. The Sunnah of the Prophet 177
2. Seven thousand pieces of gold 177
3. Respecting Prophet's heritage 179
4. Astonishing formulas proposed by the Prophet 181
5. Sending salatu salaam to the noble Prophet 187
6. Taking example of the Prophet's manner 189
7. Those who love are those who know 189
8. Observing the Prophet's sunnah in our daily lives 193

INTRODUCTION

On reading

In order to think, human beings use words. For this reason, as our vocabulary expands so does the limits of the pondering mind. This in turn increases the level of a person's intellectual capacity. One's level of intelligence is best measured by the richness of his vocabulary. Intelligence resembles a muscle, its strength increases with training and exercise. Activities such as problem solving, reading, analyzing books and listening to lectures and also increasing the vocabulary are the best forms of exercise for the mind.

Frequent reading is the most efficient way of increasing your vocabulary.

Shakespeare used 80,000 words in his books and 50,000 words were used by Goethe in his novels. Today, English and German students have no difficulty in understanding these books. This means the level of their vocabulary is adequate enough to comprehend these novels.

Unfortunately, an average university student in our schools possesses a vocabulary level of 3,000 to 4,000 words. This is purely based on our poor book reading habits. In simple terms, we do not read enough.

In the United States they conducted an experiment on intelligence levels. In the experiment, they used students from two different classes. At the beginning of the semester, intelligence levels of students from both classes were measured. During the first semester both classes were taught mathematics. At the end of the semester, the levels of intelligence were measured again and results showed that there were no significant differences. In the second semester, students in one class were asked to read certain books along with their usual lectures. The tests at the end of the semester showed that the students who read books had doubled their level of intelligence, in comparison to the other class.

The lesson we derive from the experiment is that reading books does not only enhance our vocabulary but it also affects our ability to comprehend other sciences.

During verbal examinations we are frequently assessed with literature. The test questions can be divided into three categories:

a) Paragraph questions: Usually we are given half a page to read and then we are asked 7-8 questions regarding the material we read. Those who do not have a reading habit and those who do not possess a photographic memory will easily forget what they have just read and fail to answer the questions correctly. It is usually necessary for them to read the same paragraph over and over again. This in turn decreases their ability to utilize time more efficiently.

b) Questions regarding vocabulary: In this category we are usually given certain words and asked for their synonyms and antonyms. Therefore, reading books is the best way of developing our vocabulary and enhancing our knowledge of words.

c) Questions on comprehension: These questions are given to test our ability to understand and comprehend what we have read. Once again, reading is the only way we can develop a skill to grasp and explain the topics we are given.

Why is it imperative for a student to read books?

Many volumes of books need to be written in order to describe the benefits and bounties of reading. However, let us summarize the topic with a point form reminder to those unique individuals preparing for the world of tomorrow and to those who have aims and objectives to achieve great things in life:

- James Howell states: *"Our world is governed by the pen, paper and ink"* There is no doubt that he is quite accurate in his statement. No matter which branch of employment we choose as a career, we will always be a number within the firm of our employer. Balzac says: *"In order to become the master of knowledge, one has to be a slave of work"* Being number one in life, means to possess general knowledge in many different topics. Hence, reading is the most essential thing in the process.

Another important principle on the path to success is learning from the experience of those before us and avoiding the mistakes they made in the past. Let us say, you have decided to become a computer engineer. Reading a book written by an engineer who has 20 years of experience would mean you will begin your career with 20 years of experience. We must not forget that every page we read is the product of years of experience.

Obviously, no matter which career we choose for ourselves, we have to interact with many people and provide solutions to their problems. An individual is truly successful when he/she is able to produce projects from which the entire humanity can benefit. For example, a mechanical engineer's success is measured by the amount of customers who are satisfied with the motor vehicle they purchase. One must interact with society in order to understand their needs and requirements.

- A proverb says, "A trade is a golden bracelet". A tradesman will always benefit from his profession. Even the wealthiest people could face bankruptcy. Those who hold high offices could lose their positions. However, knowledge and reputation obtained through reading will continue to subsist all the way to the grave. If you wish to obtain a status where you will never be abandoned by those around you, then you must read a lot.
- You must have heard of the saying, "Humanity is more important than wealth and rank". The word 'humanity' in the statement could be defined as maturity, honesty, kindness and politeness. These are the unique attributes of those who are loved by society. Books are the best resources for obtaining these qualities. So, if you wish to be appreciated by everyone then you need to read a lot.

One of the most significant benefits of reading is self-recognition. Through reading you will get the opportunity to know yourself and discover your talent and abilities. We must not forget that Thomas Edison, the inventor of the light globe and Albert Einstein, physicist who has won the Nobel Price were not university graduates. They discovered their own talents through the many books they read. Indeed, succeeding in life depends on our relationship with books.

There are many ways of acquiring knowledge. For example, we could attend lectures and watch documentaries. However, during a lecture we do not have the time to think and contemplate on the information that was passed onto us. Yet books always provide us ample time, hence we can always go back and read the same information over and over again. How accurate was Cicero when he stated, "A home without a book is like a body without a soul.

How does reading books support our studies?

As stated before, reading books help us to exercise our mind. Our ability to memorize things increases with reading and we enhance our vocabulary at the same time. This in turn allows us to develop our capability of comprehension.

As also indicated before, literature is one of the most important subjects in school and during examinations we are assessed on our ability to use the English language and to analyze written text. Consequently, reading books is the best way of preparing for such exams or assessments.

Reading books also help us succeed in other subjects such as physics and mathematics. Since these subjects require a mind which has the essentials to think broadly and comprise issues such as force, energy, work, motion and complex calculations, reading books will also improve one's arithmetical skills. These days, utilizing time efficiently is the most important issue during tests. This means we need to answer questions rapidly and solve problems promptly. During exams minutes are as valuable as gold, hence a student with regular reading habit will have no difficulty in understanding the questions. In conclusion, do not abstain from reading if you wish to succeed in your exams.

The type of books we should be reading

First of all, we should realize that we live in a world where even animals select the plants they consume. Hence an intelligent human being must carefully select the books he/she reads. During the process of selection, it is important to take the advice of our elders and to remember our culture and moral values so that initially we choose books that will develop our feelings of righteousness, morality and virtue. Other than this important point, we may read any book that draws our interest.

Our beloved Prophet has established a golden principle with the following statement: "I seek refuge in Allah from knowledge that has no benefit". Throughout history many civilizations have met their demise because of the simple fact that the minds' of their youth had been filled with superfluous knowledge. It is quite important to read books that satisfy both our intellect and our heart. We must never forget that human beings possess a soul, in addition to their physical bodies.

Unfortunately, the majority of our population is not in the habit of reading books. Take a good look around you, how many families that you know of have a reading habit and encourage their children to read books. Incidentally, this means we are avoiding something as essential as food and water. Parents usually make a common mistake by assuming that the text books studied in schools are enough for their children; hence they believe they have fulfilled their obligation by sending their kids to school. Perhaps, school text books provide the basic information for us to recognize our environment. How about issues regarding our own existence? Have we ever thought about our origin or our final destination? Since each day that passes by brings us closer to death, does this mean that we all resemble a person waiting on death row? Of course, as a Muslim we have answers to these questions. But, how many of us have the knowledge to answer questions put forward by a non-Muslim, regarding our faith? If we claim to believe in something, then we must certainly be able to thoroughly describe what we believe. Unfortunately, these days there are many people who claim to be Muslims yet they know very little about their own faith. So, what is more natural than a student who learns his religion by reading whilst continuing his normal studies?

Reading books

In the holy Qur'an, the Almighty Allah encourages His Prophet to say the following prayer, "O Lord, increase me in knowledge…" (Taha, 114). The mysteries of the universe, from the microcosm to the macrocosm, can only be comprehended with the knowledge that Allah bestows upon us. This is why He encourages believers to ask for knowledge through prayers. Unlike other creatures on earth, human beings are born ignorant. However, it is in our nature to constantly improve ourselves as we travel on a path to perfection. Throughout their lives, human beings struggle to understand and give meaning to the mysterious incidents that occur within their inner and external worlds. The curiosity encourages us to learn and seek answers to questions that occupy our minds. This in turn leads to a plea for help from the All-knowing, who educates and fosters us with His infinite knowledge.

One interesting aspect of the first Qur'anic revelation which begins with the commandment, *'Read'* is: According to Arabic grammar, a verse is defined as a verb. Under normal circumstances along with the verb, the subject should also contain an object. However, in this case when Allah commands us to 'read', He does not specify what we are required to read. The divine purpose for believers here is to read materials commencing with the most imperative issues of life. Beginning with religion, the circle of reading material can be expanded by studying science, literature, sociology and other subjects. With the verse above, Allah signifies the importance of reading and reminds us that there is no limit to knowledge.

Muslims who understood the essence of this Qur'anic message made amazing progress in technology and science especially during the middle ages. Franz Rosenthal made the following statement regarding the issue: "No faith system has achieved a perfect harmony between religion and science to the extent reached by Islam".

At this point we should mention some examples from the Islamic world that lead Franz Rosenthal to praise Islam.

Al Hakam, the Sultan of Andalusia sent merchants to countries far away, ordering them to purchase new books. He gave them large amounts of money so that they may find books containing new information. These books would then be brought back to Andalusia. French physicist P. Curie made the following statement: "We were able to divide the atom using the remaining 30 books from Andalusia. We would have been traveling between galaxies if only half of the million books that were destroyed had been spared."

In the beginning of the 10th century the libraries of Cordoba contained 600,000 hand written books. On the other hand, King Charles the fifth, who was the king of France at the time, had 900 books in his library. Ironically, Charles had the reputation of being Europe's most educated leader. Fascinatingly, a library in Baghdad, established by Caliph Al Ma'mun contained one million books. It is recorded that during this time approximately one third of the population of Baghdad read books.

When Ankara was captured by Harun Rashed and the Byzantium army was defeated by Caliph Ma'mun, both were offered payments. Interestingly, both Sultans requested hand written ancient scriptures instead of gold coins.

The tradition of obsession with books also continued with the Ottomans. Following many victories, the Ottomans demanded a list books from their enemies. It is recorded that during his campaign against Egypt, Sultan Selim I loaded his books on a camel and took them along.

Now, let us think about the current world. Unfortunately, as a nation we do not possess the sensitivity that our ancestors showed towards books. These days we are not interested in books, yet we prefer to acquire knowledge from TV channels that usually target the intelligence level of a fifteen year old. TV prevents people from contemplating on meaningful words. Simply because, the pictures that continuously flow from the screen divert our attention. Eventually, we are drawn away from rational thinking with special effects and sounds. Authentic knowledge cannot be obtained by being hypnotized with technological effects. It can only be achieved by reflecting on the true meaning of words.

Indeed, people like Cemil Meriç who lost his eyesight reading books day and night, and Ali Emiri Efendi, who said, "many nights, I have read books until sunrise", were aware of the facts stated above.

The minds and hearts of people of the modern world have been conquered by daily events and unproductive disputes. It is possible to save society from this unremitting deception. Initially, we must believe that education is not restricted to intellectuals and that we are all obligated to educate ourselves from cradle to grave. Perhaps in this day and age where moving pictures rule, it would be a nice idea to make the pilgrimage from the TV room to the study room where we can read. We need to make time for reading and as Balzac said, *"If we wish to become the master of knowledge, we need to be a servant of work"*.

Those who read frequently become quite noticeable. When they speak, you sense the authority, earnestness and solemnity in their tone of voice. They are never short for words and they speak with logic. Their conversation never bores anyone. The knowledge they attain through reading keeps their minds in constant action. Hence, this has a positive effect in their studies and work. They are always productive. New ideas and projects usually originate from this type of individuals.

We must then begin by reading books that attain their inspiration from the main Book, books that resurrect the soul and provide remedy to illnesses which cause defection in the hearts and minds of our generation.

A different point of view on reading

Reading is the most essential element for a human being who is on the path to self-recognition and understanding the universe. Education is the only means of preparing for life and becoming beneficial to society. However, as we prepare for the life ahead, we need to consider all of our options. It takes approximately 15 years from primary school to completing a degree in university. This is quite a long period of preparation. We must not forget that our religion mentions an eternal life which also awaits us. Whether it is positive or negative, our situation in the Hereafter depends on the life we live here. We dedicate ourselves to education here so that we can have a good life, then what kind of an enthusiasm should we possess towards knowledge that we would greatly benefit from in the everlasting life. It is imperative for a believer to question himself in relation to this issue. In our afterlife, we will be questioned about our enthusiasm towards worldly knowledge and be asked why we have not displayed the same eagerness towards learning our religion. In order to avoid this kind of questioning, we must thoroughly read and study our religion. There is no doubt that death is a reality and it is imminent. Consequently, one must also prepare himself for the hereafter with knowledge and good deeds.

Last word

We have learned some information regarding the benefits of reading; let us now take a look at some unique examples:

Towards the end of 1945 Japan was a devastated country. Today however, Japan has made so much progress that economically it has the power to overcome the USA. There are many reasons for this. Here is an example; one newspaper in Japan has a daily distribution of 11 million copies whilst the total distribution of all newspapers in Turkey is about 4 million copies. Regrettably, we do not read enough.

It is recorded that when the Ottoman Sultan Selim I was a prince, he would sleep 3 hours a day allocating 8 hours to reading. According to a survey conducted in Turkey with 5139 youths, 69% could not remember the title of the last book they read. Lenin, who established the foundations of Communist Russia, read Marks' book a thousand times under the freezing conditions of Siberia. What about us? We are the heir of a magnificent civilization, yet take a good look at our reading habits. How much are we reading and are we able to transfer our knowledge into action? Isn't it time that we question ourselves in relation to this issue.

CHAPTER ONE

1. Signs in the window

Every masterpiece points to art and an act of designing. A poem points to poetry, building points to construction and a song points to music. Consequently, all types of art and design point to a designer which exists at their foundation. Great places of worship such as the Taj Mahal and the Blue Mosque illustrate a perfect architecture. Titles such as architect, designer, painter, embroiderer, and musician, are given to individuals for the talent they possess. These talents in turn indicate to those with exceptional abilities and to souls nourished with inspiration. Indeed, it would be quite absurd to deny the architect of the Blue Mosque after beholding its beauty or to reject the unique talent behind the design of Pyramids. What logic is there in not recognizing the artist who painted Mona Lisa? Can we claim that there is no poet behind a poem?

Using the examples above, when we observe the masterpiece and beauty that exists in the universe and in nature, we realize that there is design, architecture, harmony, laws and regulations, art and poetry. This in turn points to certain titles and names of a designer. These titles and names then indicate to unique attributes of perfection. Finally, these attributes of perfection then point to a Supreme Being whose Grace is at the point of perfection and whose perfection is defined as the All-Gracious. This reality is so evident that it is visible even to blind eyes.

Most certainly, all creatures point to unique acts of design and all acts of design point to exalted names and attributes, hence all of the Glorious Names and Attributes point to an All-Knowing, All-Powerful and All-Gracious Being.

Oh denying carnal soul! How will you explain the brilliant testimonies that fill the entire universe? Do you possess the power to silence these witnesses?

2. Can a bridge build itself?

Imam-ı Azam Abu Hanifa is one the greatest Islamic scholars. Those who follow him in matters of practice are called Hanafi. Even as a child, Imam-ı Azam possessed a brilliant mind. One day, a stranger came to Baghdad, where Abu Hanifa lived when he was a child. This man had great confidence in himself. He asked who in Baghdad can prove the existence of God. People pointed at Abu Hanifa, and replied:

– Our young scholar can prove the existence of Allah.

The arrogant man glanced at young Abu Hanifa and said:

– Let us see you do it then.

A large curious audience gathered. Then the man climbed to a high platform. He was arrogantly staring at everyone from a high position, whilst bragging about his knowledge. At that point, Abu Hanifa said, "I left my books at home. I need to go and get them."

So they gave him permission to go home. However, he was gone for a long time and people began to feel uncomfortable about their choice. "We should have found another opponent for this arrogant man" they said. However, everyone somehow sensed that there was something unusual here, since Abu Hanifa had never broken his word before.

A fair amount of time had gone by hence the crowd became restless. Suddenly, the young Imam appeared. There was a sense of relief felt by everyone. On the other hand, the confidence of the man was booming as he asked: "Where were you all this time? Perhaps you realized that you cannot prove the existence of Allah."

Abu Hanifa replied calmly: "I have no doubt about Allah and proving his existence is quite easy. However, I live on the other side of the river that flows from the centre of Baghdad. I ran into a small problem on my way back. A sudden storm had blown all the boats away and the bridge had collapsed.

– Then how did you manage to get across, asked, the man.

– I will explain. As I came near the banks of the river, I saw large boulders rolling down into the river. They were falling into perfect positions to form the foundations of a bridge. Later, pieces of timber fell randomly from the sky and lined up on the foundations. And then, amazingly, nails appeared from nowhere and began to join the timbers piercing through like arrows. At the end of this remarkable series of events, there I was standing in front of a perfect bridge. So I crossed over and here I am.

As everyone listened to the incredible story in shock and disappointment, the man asked in an ironic tone:

– Couldn't you find someone smarter than this little boy? I do not have time for this nonsense!

– What part of my story is nonsense, replied Abu Hanifa.

– All of it...How can a bridge be constructed without a builder or a laborer, asked the man.

– Then permit me to ask you; what is more complex in design, a bridge or the entire world, replied Abu Hanifa.

– The world of course...it is much bigger and more complex in design.

Now it was Abu Hanifa's turn to respond. "You claim that a bridge, which is much easier to build, must have an architect and a builder. Then how can you claim that this astonishing planet has no designer or an architect?

The man was stunned by the reply as he attempted to reserve his composure. Then he replied: "Very well, I accept that this earth must have been created by someone."

– Of course, and that someone is Allah, said Abu Hanifa.

The man was cornered now. Assuming he still had some valid points of argument, he asked:

– If Allah exists, then how come we do not see him?

Abu Hanifa smiled, as if he had found the question too easy and then replied:

– Let us have some warm milk and relax first. Then I will answer your question.

The glasses of milk had arrived and both individuals added some honey to sweeten their milk. Then Abu Hanifa took another spoon full of honey and said, "Let me add this into your milk to make it sweet". The man replied, "Thanks, I have already added some honey to my milk, I want you to answer my question first". Once again Abu Hanifa repeated his offer insistently, "Let me first add some sweetener into your milk". By now the man had lost his temper as he shouted:

– I told you, I have already added sweetener to my milk!

– I do not believe you, replied Abu Hanifa.

– Why do you not believe me, shouted, the man.

– Because I cannot believe something I do not see.

– Obviously, you cannot see the sweetener in the milk because it is all ready mixed in it. You would have to taste the milk to detect it. Tell me why are you keeping me occupied with this sort of thing? Answer my question first.

Abu Hanifa smiled and commenced his argument:

– I have already answered it. Indeed, you cannot see the sweetener that has already mixed into the milk, but you can detect its existence by tasting the milk. Obviously, we are unable to see Allah, but we can perceive His existence through His creation. When we apply our senses to all occurrences that take place in the universe, then we will discover the hand of God behind all of them. As you see, you cannot even observe a simple sweetener with your eyes when it is mixed into the milk, yet you wish to behold God. If you wish to see Allah, then I suggest you use the eye of your intelligence, not your limited sight.

The man had nowhere to go now. He was devastated by defeat. You could see that he was in agony, searching for another question. He thought for awhile and then said:

– Alright... I have one last question for you. I accept that Allah exists and that we cannot see Him. Then tell me, this God that we cannot see but realize with our intelligence. What is He doing right now?

Abu Hanifa looked at the man and said:

– This is also a simple question; however, I need to answer it from where you are now.

The man was confused as he stood up on the high platform then made his way down. Then Abu Hanifa climbed onto the same platform and replied:

– Allah the Almighty has brought an unbeliever such as yourself, down from this platform and replaced him with a young believer like me.

As a result, the man accepted Islam.

3. Various evidences regarding the existence of Allah

a) The universe is not eternal: According to the second law of thermo-dynamics, there is a constant energy loss in the universe. This means that the differences in heat, pressure and density tend to even out in a closed physical system. Eventually, these entities will also even out in our universe and this in turn will bring the universe to an energetic death. If the universe was eternal, this process would have already completed its cycle. So, the second law of thermo-dynamics suggests that the universe had a beginning.

b) Electrons: Electrons that exist in matter are in constant motion. These motions cause continuous alterations in the structure of matter. If matter was eternal, these alterations would also have already completed their cycles. In addition to this, latest research in particle physics proves that all sub-atomic particles have a lifespan. In conclusion, matter is not eternal.

c) In our sun, 564 million tons of hydrogen is being converted to helium each second. This means that our sun is becoming denser whilst each minute it loses 240 million tons from its mass. It is calculated that the average lifespan of a star is ten billion years. There are billions of stars in the universe. If the universe was eternal, all of these stars would have completed their cycles and died out. This means that the universe had a beginning.

As you see, physical laws such as thermo-dynamics and research in the field of astrophysics prove that matter is not eternal.

4. Is it possible that matter came into existence by chance?

Let us assume that we have three books in a room. Each book has a number on the front cover and they are placed on a table in sequence of 1, 2, and 3. There is no one but a blind child in this room. Can we consider the possibility that the blind child has placed them in the correct order and without any help? What if we increase the number of books to 20?

Let us say that a printer has half a million set of letters. If someone comes up to you claiming that a strong wind blew these letters off the table and by chance we found three words on the floor, formed by the letters (Rock, Salt and Lake). Although the probability is quite low, you may choose to accept the possibility. What if we claim that a whole article consisting of astounding poetry was formed by a mere chance? Would you still consider believing such a story?

Let us say we wrote numbers from 1 to 10 on small pieces of paper and randomly threw them on the floor. The probability of these numbers lining up from 1 to 10 is 10 billion to 1. If we increase the number to 12, then the probability becomes 100 billion to 1. When the number of papers is raised to 22, the probability is 100 billion x 100 billion to 1.

It is impossible for a blind person to line up 20 books in a sequence corresponding to their numbers. It is impossible for a printing machine to produce a book by coincidence. Then how can we even assume that a masterpiece such as the book of the universe, flowers with their amazing colors and magnificent scents, animals with incredible talents and beautiful designs, human beings with their miraculously complex biological structures and galaxies and stars that move with precision and harmony are all products of a blind chance.

"There is Order and Harmony in the Universe, Not Chance, and Allah is the Implementer of This Order."

5. Rights of a mother and father

Mothers and Fathers are sanctified beings who should be respected accordingly. Disrespecting them is regarded as same as disrespecting God. Those who harass their parents will soon be harassed accordingly.

Human beings become a burden on their parents from the day they begin to develop as an embryo. No one can understand the agony and hardship that parents go through in raising their children with love and compassion. Their compassion cannot be measured in relation to this mater. For this reason, respecting them is not only a duty but a debt all of us must repay.

Those who realize the value of their parents and think of them as a means to attract God's mercy are the most fortune in both worlds. However, those who think of them as a burden and find their existence as unbearable are evil nominees for eternal punishment.

The degree of one's respect to God can be measured by his respect towards his parents. It is an unfortunate thing that these days even those who claim to love God are rebelling against their parents.

A person should be obedient and extremely respectful towards his parents, and in turn a mother and father should display the same compassion for their child's soul and heart, as they do for his physical being. This means that they should place their child in the trustworthy hands of the most experienced instructors and teachers. Parents that disregard the soul and heart of their children are the most ignorant and a child who is a victim of this negligence is the most unfortunate.

A person who ignores the rights of his parents transforms into a hideous being and parents who refrain from establishing a spiritual life for their children are merciless tyrants. How about those parents who try to paralyze the life of their child who has already found the right path? Families are the foundations of society. A harmonious society depends on its families and the respect displayed within these nucleus communities. If compassion and respect is no longer exists in a family, who could expect to find them in the society.

6. A mother's heart

Once upon a time, a young man fell in love with a girl who had a heart of stone. One day, she came up with a horrific suggestion. "I will test your love. Bring me your mother's heart then I shall marry you" she said. The young man trembled upon hearing this horrendous ultimatum. He walked away thinking, "there is no way I would do such a thing". But as days passed by, he realized that he could not live without her. So, he decided to prove himself. As he walked towards his mother with a knife in his hand, she made no attempt to stop him. The young man murdered his mother and removed her heart placing it in a handkerchief. He was full of excitement as he began to run towards the girl's house. Suddenly, he tripped over a rock and fell on his knees. The heart rolled out of his hands. It was still fresh. In tremendous pain, the young man screamed:

"Oh Mum!" Abruptly, a voice echoed from the heart: "My son... did you hurt yourself!"

7. Compassion of mothers

"Can I see my baby", said the young mother who had recently given birth to a baby boy. Taking the baby from the nurse she embraced him with great enthusiasm and compassion. However, the mother was frozen like an iceberg when she opened the cloth to see her baby's face. The doctor and the nurse had turned their faces away both were staring at the window. The newborn had no ears. Examinations showed that this would not affect his hearing, and that the only problem was his physiological appearance.

Many years had gone by and the child started school. One day, he came home and threw himself in his mother's arms. He was crying his eyes out. "One of the big kids called me a freak", he muttered as he wept.

The unfortunate child grew up with this burden. He was a bright young man who could have been very successful if only he could socialize with others. His parents were deeply concerned and felt his pain in their hearts. One day the father asked the family doctor if there was something they could do. The doctor said, "The only solution is an organ donor"

The young man was happy, but who would sacrifice their ears? Two years later, one sunny day, the parents gave the good news, "get ready son, we are going to the hospital. Your mother and I found you a suitable donor who wishes that his identity be kept a secret"

The operation was a great success. Finally, the young man had ears. His confidence grew each day and he was extremely successful in school and in his social life. After completing his education, he got married and became a diplomat. Many years had passed and one day he asked his father, "Please dad, tell me the identity of this wonderful person who gave me a chance in life".

"I am sorry son, but we had a deal and I cannot reveal this person's identity to you".

The identity of the donor was hidden from him for many years, until the saddest day in his life had arrived. He had lost his mother. They were all standing by her lifeless body at the funeral. His father approached the body of his beloved wife and began to stroke her hair. As he pushed her dark brown hair towards the back of her head, the son noticed that her ears were missing.

The father then turned towards his son and said, "Your mum never needed a haircut, hence no one could question her beauty".

Yes, the real beauty is in your heart not on your skin. True happiness is not found on things you see, but in places you do not see. Perhaps, real love and compassion is hidden in things that we are not aware of...

8. Manners

In general, manners could be described as: Controlling one's behavior and words in accordance to universal morals and etiquettes. In this regard, speaking to a person who requests knowledge from you and keeping quite next to a scholar is considered as good manners. Yes, from sitting to standing, laughing to crying, all types of behavior which is done appropriately can be regarded as good manners.

Parents are the primary teachers of good manners. A child enters society with the manners obtained from his/her parents. This behavior begins to take shape by the positive or negative influence exerted at school and in the community. We must not forget that a child who has received good manners from the family will preserve his/her composure contrary to all persuasions.

Islamic scholars always point out to the fact that you cannot have faith and knowledge in the absence of good manners. There is no doubt that developing good manners is the first step in studying religion and other sciences.

9. Respecting our teachers

During his stay in Basra they saw that Sahl b. Abdullah had a bandage on his finger. When he was asked about it, he said that he felt some pain in his finger.

Sometime later, one of the persons who were present went to Egypt and decided to visit the great scholar Zunnun-i Misri. He realized that he had also bandaged his finger. Curiously, he asked the same question to Zunnun-i Misri. He replied: "My finger has been sore for quite a long time". The man realized why Sahl had also bandaged his finger; it was out of respect for his teacher.

One morning, a few years after the incident, Sahl came next to his students. He was quite calm and relaxed as he leaned on the wall and stretched his legs. He said, "Ask me any question you wish". They were all shocked because they had never seen their teacher behave like this. Hence, they could not hold back as they asked, "We have never seen you like this, did something change?"

"One must take extreme care with his manners as long as his teacher is living", he replied.

That day, his students learned that Zunnun-i Misri had passed away.

10. How did they correct a wrong?

Hasan and Husayn, the grandchildren of the noble Prophet were at the mosque one day, watching an old man performing Wudu.

At one stage, Hasan said to his brother:

– Did you see that, he did not wash his elbows?

– Yes, he also left some other parts out, replied Husayn.

– We have to warn him that his Wudu will not be valid if he leaves out the parts that we are obligated to wash. Even an area, size of a pin's head should not be neglected. Obviously, his prayer will also be invalid without a correct ablution.

– But how can we say this to him? Look, he also neglected his toes, and forgot to wash his heals.

Husayn:

– Wait...he is an old man; he would be embarrassed if we tried to correct his mistakes. Or he might not even take us seriously, because we are kids. I have an idea!

Husayn then walked up to the old man and said:

– Sir, we need your assistance with something.

– Alright kids tell me what you want, said the old man.

– We are still young and we fear that we might make a mistake when we perform our Wudu. Could you please watch us and correct our mistakes?

– Ok then, go ahead, replied the old man.

Both Hasan and Husayn began to perform their Wudu. The old man was watching them carefully, looking for an error. However, they performed their Wudu so flawlessly that the man thought of his own Wudu and realized that he was the one with the mistakes. Then with an assuring smile on his face, he stroked their hair and said:

– You are not the ones with mistakes. It is me. I would like to thank you for reminding me in such a kind manner. From this day on, I will perform my Wudu as you do.

Dear young man, as you see knowing something is not enough, what is more important is to pass the knowledge on in an appropriate manner, without breaking anyone's heart. Just as the grandchildren of the Prophet did...

CHAPTER TWO

1. A cell will tell

The phenomenon of cells with different structures and functions coming together to form living tissues, organs and biological beings with complex mechanisms.

Epithelium cells are the most basic tissues in the human body, yet they operate like a chemical factory in order to identify the most beneficial molecules from the thousands of nutritional molecules that enter the body.

How about those white blood cells being able to change their structure in order to recognize and fight 30,000 various types of molecules.

What about the Neuron cells that exist in our brains and their capability of performing tasks more than a million computers?

Isn't it amazing that thousands of cells which form the walls of the heart contracts the whole muscle by generating tension, as they behave like a single cell?

The requirements of a cell situated at the most distant part of the body is detected by the chemistry of our blood and necessary hormones are released in order to satisfy its need.

All of these amazing functions and vital tasks are preserved by genetic codes and passed over generations. From living tissues to immense galaxy systems, everything points to a magnificent order that functions with precision and harmony.

All we have to do is to open our eyes and observe the amazing order which governs all matter from atoms to galaxies. There is no doubt that the billions of microscopic cells that function together like an organized army in order to serve and protect the body in which they exist. This clearly indicates to a magnificent plan, program and design.

This astonishing plan and program, then points to a great programmer who governs all matter.

Think of all the green plants and how they were designed to clear the air in order to protect us from the deadly carbon-dioxide that we release into the atmosphere. Isn't it the very same plants that rush to our aid by providing minerals, vitamins and nutrition in their branches and roots? How about those animals that consume green plants so that they could synthesize proteins in order to offer us meat? As you see, the food chain in nature was established for the benefit of human beings. Even the carcasses of animals are decomposed into earth with the help of bacteria in order to protect the ecosystem and to prevent waste.

Most certainly, the inexplicable function of plants, animals and matter and also the mysterious way in which they are preserved and governed to serve a common purpose, indicates to a miraculous program. Hence, this amazing program clearly points to the existence of a programmer.

The way that the entire universe is designed with perfect organization and harmonious order, and that all matter, from atoms to galaxies moving according to a program, bear witness to the Exalted Being Who brightens everything from the human face to the heavens above.

2. The unity whispered by the animals

A honey bee collects pollen from thousands of flowers. Then finds its direction by using the ultraviolet rays emitted by the sun. Later, just like an architect, it constructs a container made up of perfect geometrical shapes, in which it will produce its honey. Where does the honey bee get the knowledge to find its way using the sun? Who teaches it the technique of finding the correct flowers? How did it learn to make honey and how does an insect with no intelligence perform these incredible tasks? A mosquito begins to bite as soon as it has learned to fly. Where did it get the knowledge about the benefits of human blood? As soon as it's threatened, it makes a getaway, using sophisticated maneuvers, how did it develop the skills of a professional pilot? Sea eels make the great journey traveling through oceans to lay their eggs at a location situated south of Bermuda. Then they all travel back to the region which they originally came from, such as the Mediterranean Sea, Indian Ocean and so on. Once, all the eggs are hatched, the young eels travel to the region of their parents. How do they know where to go and find their way back through great oceans without intelligence, a map or a compass? Hens sit on their eggs during the incubation period. Excluding the 1st and the 20th day, every day they flip their eggs around. Originally, scientists thought that this was done to control the heat so that it is distributed evenly. However, the prototype incubator they had built to disburse heat evenly did not work. Sometime later, an interesting discovery was made. All the protein deposits were being gathered at the bottom of the egg hence it needed to be turned around so that proteins could be distributed evenly. In which chemical laboratory did the chicken study these crucial details? And how did it teach these scientific facts to its generation?

A type of wasp lays its eggs in a nest constructed at the size of a walnut. Then it flies away to find food. Sometime later it returns with a grasshopper it has captured. The grasshopper is still alive yet in a stage of coma. The queen has released her venom in calculated amounts so that its victim remains in a coma. This is done to preserve the food for 20 days, during which its young will come out of the larva stage. The young wasps never meet their mother, yet they follow exactly the same procedure when it is time for them to lay eggs. Are wasps anesthetic experts? Where did they study medicine?

When certain bird species are terminated, snake populations increase. When snakes are killed, frog populations increase. And when frogs are destroyed, the fly population increases. Who establishes this amazing balance in nature?

Bats are blind, they find their way around by using a radar system we call echo-location. It works by sound waves that bounce off objects and return to the bat's sensors. Scientists invented the radar by simulating bats. We are amazed by the technology of radars yet we do not even take the time to think about its origin, the bat.

3. Examples from humans

When we feel cold, our body begins to shiver. This is a biological reaction sending a signal to our circulatory system to pump blood more rapidly. Human beings have no control over this. Then who designed this magnificent system?

During summer our body temperature increases. This in turn causes our skin to excrete sweat. Sweat is excreted from our skin in order to cool the body down. However, during winter our blood vessels narrow down in order to preserve heat. Who is the designer of this astonishing biological thermo-control system?

During sleep, we change our position several times. This is done unconsciously to avoid being paralyzed. The turning function is controlled by the nose. Within our nasal cavities there are two unique compartments in which a special liquid flows from one side to the other. It takes approximately 45 minutes for the liquid to flow from one compartment to the other. Once the compartment is full, a message is sent to ours brains, and then the brain goes into action asking the body to change its position. Our nose also has the ability to identify and distinguish 10,000 different scents. It controls the temperature of the air that enters our lungs and stomach keeping it around 32.2 degrees. During summer when the outside temperature raises to 35 degrees, the temperature within the nose automatically drops to about minus 3. And during winter the process is reversed in extremely cold conditions, bringing the inner temperature of the nose all the way up to 35 degrees. How about the mucus that captures bacteria that enters the body using the respiratory system? Isn't it obvious that we are constantly being protected by a mysterious but most merciful hand?

A breathtaking painting signifies a talented artist. What about the colorful designs we observe on animals and plants, do they not remind us of a great artist?

4. Everything points to God

A Baby fish asked its mother, "What is water, can you show it to me?"

The mother fish replied, "My dear child, show me something other than water, then I'll tell you what water is".

Sometimes, you come across intellectuals who claim that they do not understand the existence of God simply because they cannot see Him. How can an intelligent person wish to see God when the human eyesight is quite limited? It is a fact that we are unable to see most of His creation, yet we expect to see Him. The only way that we can observe God is through His creation. We see God by using our intelligence hence without God the entire universe would have no meaning. So, in this case just as the mother fish, we say, "Show me something that is not His creation, then I'll show you God.

5. Why cannot we see God?

The answer to this question will be quite similar to an answer we would give to a student who asks during an exam, "Why can't we see the answers on the exam sheet". Yes, we are also being tested on this earth and this is the main reason why we cannot see God. Giving the answers to all students during an exam would mean injustice to those that have studied for days and nights, and an unfair advantage to those that have not studied at all. Just as the analogy, if we were allowed to see certain things that we are meant to have faith in, examination in this life would have no meaning. This means the good and the bad would not have been separated, life on earth would have no meaning and the creation of Heaven and Hell would have been unnecessary.

Let us ask ourselves, what percent of the world are we able to see? Forget about the world, are we even capable of seeing the entire city in which we live? When we question our ability to see, we realize that our sight is restricted to a level that observes perhaps only the one billionth of the universe. This is only a tiny fraction of the universe, yet we wish to observe its creator. Denying the existence of God is as ludicrous as denying our own existence.

We will continue with another analogy. There are approximately, 5 million red blood cells in a millimeter cube of blood. Let us say that one of these blood cells has been influenced by an anarchist bacterium and begins to claim, "I do not believe that human beings exist because I cannot see them". This would be quite an ironic statement since this tiny microscopic being lives inside the human body. Now, let us take a look at the flip side of the coin; in size, human beings are millions of times larger than a blood cell and possess intelligence. On the other hand, we are billions of times smaller than the universe we live in. How foolish would it be for a human being to deny God simply because he/she cannot see the Creator of the universe?

6. Status of belief

A group of people had gathered to learn knowledge from a renowned scholar. A nonbeliever who happened to be passing by decided to join them. His intentions were to create confusion in their minds by asking questions which he thought the scholar could not answer. He approached the scholar and said, "Sir, there are some questions which have been bothering me for quite sometime now...can you please enlighten me?" The scholar invited him to speak.

First of all, you people claim that Satan was created out of fire, yet you say he will be punished in fire. How could fire burn fire?

My second question; you say that God creates both good and evil. Then how can he punish a sinner when it was God himself who created his sins?

Lastly, you say that God is present everywhere then shouldn't he be here right now? Can you show him to me?

The scholar placed his hand on his chin and thought for awhile. Then he glanced around as if he was looking for something. Finally, he had found what he was looking for, a hard piece of clay. Quickly, he grabbed it and hit the man over the head. The scholar shouted, "Here is your answer! The man was in shock as he grabbed his bleeding head in agony and left the scene.

A short while after the incident, they were both summoned to appear before a judge. The judge questioned the scholar. "If you are a scholar, then why didn't you answer his questions appropriately instead of assaulting him? The scholar replied, "That was my answer your honor". "What kind of an answer is this?" asked the judge.

The scholar replied:

– Allow me to explain. His first question was, how could fire burn fire, claiming that Satan could not feel pain in hell because he is made up of fire. So, I demonstrated to him that this was possible by striking a human being who is made up of clay with a piece of clay.

His second question was that if God creates good and evil then people are not guilty of their actions. Then may I ask, why I was summoned to a court room? If he is sincere about his claim then why did he lodge a complaint against me? According to his beliefs, I am an innocent human being. Well, in reality even he knows that this is not true, because human beings possess freewill; hence they have the freedom of choice. Whether they choose good or evil, this is up to them. Their choice, however, is created by Allah, for the purpose of the test. Consequently, we will be held accountable for our decisions. This means that Allah creates good and evil but we are the ones that make the choice.

With his last question, he claims that he cannot see God, therefore He does not exist. God has gifted us with eyes and a brain. There are things which we observe with our eyes and others with our brains. For example, he claims that he is in pain now; can he show this pain to us? Should we assume that he is not feeling any pain because we cannot see it? However, if we use our logic, we shall find a sign. One sign of his pain is the blood on his head. Now, take a good look at the universe, there are millions of signs everywhere. Turning a blind eye to all the signs and claiming that "I do not see God, therefore He does not exist", is madness.

7. Essence of friendship

Those who glorify their friends gain many defenders against their enemies. Our need for a loyal friend is no less than our need for other necessities of life. A person who is content with his friends and companions has also achieved a life of peace and contentment.

A smart person is one who renews his friendship and resolves issues as soon as conflict and problems occur. What is more preferable than this is to display total care with our relationships and preserve harmony amongst our friends.

A continuous love and relationship amongst friends depends on the understanding displayed during righteous and appropriate activities. The friendship of those who are not willing to sacrifice for each other, will not last.

The level of one's friendship could be measured by the degree of his sensitivity shown towards the joy and despair of his friend. Those who do not feel joy with their friends and do not weep when their friends suffer are not genuine friends.

True friendship becomes evident when one stands by his friend in times of misery and hardship. Those who are absent in times of adversity and desolation cannot be considered as friends.

Those who continuously argue and generate conflicts in their environment will not have many friends. If you wish to have loyal friends, then you must avoid entering into unnecessary arguments.

First of all, friendship is an issue that concerns the heart. Those who believe that they can make friends through deception and dishonesty will be disillusioned. Even if they manage to gather a temporary group of ignorant flatterers and buffoons, their friendship won't be permanent.

8. It is difficult to repair a broken heart

There was a teenager who had a bad character. One day his father gave him a wooden board and a bag of nails, and said, "Each time you have a dispute with your friends, I want you to hammer a nail into this board."

The next day, the teen had already hammered 37 nails into the board. Within the following few weeks he managed to control his behavior, and only hammered a few nails, until one day he did not need nails anymore.

He rushed to his father and showed him the board with joy. Then the father said, "From now on, you will pull out a nail for each day you spend without a fight". Many days went by and one evening the teen came running to his father. "Look father, all the nails are out!" he shouted. The young man was quite pleased with his achievement. However, his father picked up the board and said, "You did good and I am proud of you. But take a look at this board; see all the holes you made in it? It will never be the same again."

When we argue or fight with our friends, it is possible that sometimes we say bad things and each word leaves a mark (hole) in their heart. Even if your friend says that he has forgiven you a thousand times, these holes will never be closed. A good friend is like a precious diamond. He makes you laugh, gives you courage, and listens to your problems and opens his heart to you.

9. Trust

During his campaign at Mt Taurus, Alexander had fallen ill. He was so ill that he could not even stand up. He had a very high temperature and everyone believed that he would not survive. His doctor and a childhood friend prepared a powerful medicine and was about to give it to him when a soldier brought a letter for Alexander. Alexander read the message which warned him about drinking the medicine, suggesting that the doctor was bribed by the Persians to poison the King. Alexander had great trust in his companions and drank the medicine without any hesitation.

A few minutes later, he handed the letter over to his doctor and said, "I have never doubted you, not even for a minute". A few days later, he recovered and continued his campaign.

10. Humanity

Human beings should always use their conscience as a scale to balance their behavior and attitude. We should also wish upon others things that we wish upon ourselves. Hence we should never expect others to be pleased with things that we are not fond of. This way we can prevent ourselves from misconduct and breaking the hearts of others.

We get pleasure out of the good that people do for us, in return we show love and respect towards them. Accordingly, the key to earning love and respect is to do good for others. "Human beings are slaves of benevolence". Therefore, taking refuge in good is the best form of protection from those who bear evil intentions.

A person's maturity and perfection can be measured by his righteousness and good behavior even towards those who have wronged him. Yes, one should not move away from compassion and humanity even when he deals with those who have been bad to him. Retaliation to evil with evil is a grave mistake. On the other hand, displaying compassion towards those who have been bad is a form of gallantry and noble-heartedness.

There are no limits to helping others. A true philanthropist can even be generous enough to sacrifice his soul for others. However, such courage can only be authentic if the person is sincere, genuine and abstains from racialist and bigoted behavior.

A person's munificence, generosity and philanthropy can only be validated by the degree of his relation with his relatives and friends. Those who abandon their relatives and friends and claim to be generous and pure-hearted are in denial. Deserting your family and friends and claiming that they had deserved it would be considered as a sign of having a carnal soul that has not found the truth.

The greatest good you could do to people is to close your eyes to their mistake and faults. Searching for people's mistakes is an act of rudeness; gossiping about their faults is inexcusable behavior and degrading them by reminding them of the mistakes they had made can be considered as a harsh blow on the bonds of brotherhood. Alas, it is impossible for such egos to come together to form unity.

Those who consider the biggest good they have done to others as insignificant, and the smallest good that was done to them as a major thing, are contented souls who has achieved maturity in their conscience and has risen to a level of divine morality. These individuals do not remind people of the good they do, nor do they complain about the way they have been treated.

11. Being human

He was appointed to another location. The papers indicating to his relocation had arrived a week ago. This was the city where he began his career as a governor hence he was saddened by the thought of leaving. As he watched the movers load the truck with his belongings, he remembered the day he came here. It was four years ago and the governor before him had also lived in the very same building. The emotional scenes were no different as the previous governor had difficulty even when they were shaking hands. Now, it was his turn. There were many people present and some of them were weeping. He was about to leave everyone behind as he prepared to move with his family. Briefly, he thought about all the good memories, when suddenly he heard a voice. It was the old war veteran who had fought during the liberation of his country. "What is the matter with you son?" asked the war veteran. "I feel sad leaving this city" replied the governor. The old war veteran had realized that this wasn't the real reason behind his grief; hence he asked again, "I know that you are worried about something else so go ahead and tell me". The governor replied, "I have been here for four years and interacted with many people. I do not see most of them here today. I remember the day that the previous governor left, this house was full of people who came to see him off". The old war veteran had a somber smile on his face as he replied:

– Look son, it is obvious that you have educated yourself and succeeded in life by becoming a governor. If you looked down on people, avoided greeting them with a smile, and if you did not love the youth and respected the old, what else did you expect? It does not matter whether you become a governor or a king; you must become a human being first.

The governor was in shock, the old veteran had spoken quite bluntly. Quickly, he stood up and grabbed the old man's hand. He replied, "I appreciate your advice, you have taught me that being a governor isn't everything" and then kissed his hand. The governor had a sad smile on his face as he continued, "From this day on, I will take more care in my interactions with the people". The old man was pleased as he also stood up and replied, "If you want the love and respect of others, then be good to them."

12. To become a refined human being

It was past midnight. As the old man scurried through the dark streets, his disappointment was quite evident by the way he was breathing. Suddenly, he stopped for a moment, thinking about the past. It was many years ago when his son was only fourteen. Although he had sacrificed a lot so that his son could receive a good education, he was never pleased with his attitude. He even remembered the day when he pulled him aside and said, "Son, you will never become a fine, upstanding man". Many years had gone by since the incident. That night he was summoned by his son. So the old man proceeded to the office of their new governor.

As he entered the office, his son, the new governor stood up and said, "Remember father, you said that I would never become a refined man. But look at me now, I am the governor". The old man replied, "Yes son, you have indeed assumed the position of a governor, but still you have not become a human being. If you were a good man, you would not have dragged an old man from his home in the middle of the night. Instead, you would have been kind and considerate. You would have shrunk as your position grew. Yes, you have succeeded in becoming a governor but you have failed in achieving maturity." The old man was quite furious as he slammed the door and walked out. He felt miserable and guilty as he believed that he had failed to raise a well-mannered son. How much he had wished that his son would be a role-model, and a symbol of decency.

However, it wasn't meant to be. Yet he still prayed for him, "May Allah grant well-manners to him" he said.

13. Morals

During the Ottoman era they had charity walls. These walls had small compartments, in which the wealthy placed some money. To the astonishment of Western visitors, the poor would walk up to the wall and take only the amount they needed, leaving the rest for others. Also there were inns constructed by foundations to accommodate travelers. Travelers would be provided with free accommodation, food and even their horses were taking care of for three days. Within each room a bag full of money was placed by the bedside and those who needed it would take out the necessary amount leaving the rest for others who may be in need.

Those days, the term, "close the door" was never used. Instead, they would say, "cover the door". This was out of respect, because they did not wish Allah to close His door of mercy on anyone. Closing doors in a delicate manner was part of their ethics.

They also never used the term, "put the light out" because light also meant *Nur* and they did not wish Allah to take away His *Nur* from anyone. The term they used those days was, "give the lamp a rest". They never shook people in order to wake them up and never screamed their name out when they were asleep. The terminology used for waking people up was, "awaken and be aware".

Kindness, benevolence, compassion and consideration were essential in their society. They never cut people off when they spoke, they did not whisper or use hand gestures, and speaking behind people's back was unforgivable behavior.

They did not drag their feet as they walked and abstained from making loud noises. They took great care to avoid stepping on ants and insects. There were many people in society who would not even harm a fly.

Those days, as people stepped out the door they turned around to face those still in the room. Even the shoes placed in the doorway faced the house. This meant that "Although you are leaving, your feet faces our home so that you may come again" on the contrary they believed that if you faced the shoes the other way around, it meant, "you are not welcome anymore".

Yes, the people of that era lived their lives in purity, thoughtfulness and vividness...

The people of those days lived their lives as if they were beholding God. They never preferred anyone over Him; hence Allah was always on their mind. They always behaved accordingly in the presence of the Sultan of eternity and infinity. Are we not always in the presence of Allah, no matter where we go?

CHAPTER THREE

1. Arguments against faith

The arguments put forward by nonbelievers can be listed in three main categories.
- Matter exists because of a blind chance and random events
- It created itself
- It is nature, everything is created by nature

Once these arguments are refuted, nothing else can be said regarding the existence of God.

A. Everything is created by chance or a series of random events

Matter we observe in nature cannot come together by means of random events or chance. Let us prove this impossibility with a few analogies:

Let us think about a large pharmacy where hundreds of various chemicals are stored. To prepare a certain medicine, you need to mix different chemicals in correct dosages. Imagine a medicine that transforms into a deadly poison if you increased the dosage by one milligram. Now, let us assume that someone told you there were only two possible ways of preparing this medicine.

The first possibility: The containers in which the chemicals are stored were placed on a shelf. One night, a strong wind coming through the window blew the shelf down. All the containers were broken and the chemicals had splattered on the floor. But, by some bizarre coincidence, chemicals were mixed up in precise dosages and the medicine we needed was formed.

The second possibility: Professional chemists used accurate measurements to mix the correct dosage in order to prepare the medicine. In this case, which possibility would you choose to believe, random events preparing a perfect medicine or an intelligent person who has a master's degree in chemistry?

If we placed some meat, firewood and a box of matches next to each other and waited for the wind to blow and by chance light our fire and cook our meal, we would starve to death. Even the grandchildren of our grandchildren won't live to see this meal cook. Those who claim that random causes and coincidences have the ability to create should attempt to cook their meal using the method above.

B. Matter creates itself

The human body is like a palace. It is even more perfect than any palace in the world. Would anyone believe that a palace could build itself? Then how can we possibly accept an argument that claims an amazing system such as the human body creates itself.

Take a look at the blood which flows through our arteries like water through a river bed. In our blood vessels there are two types of blood cells and two types of very important proteins.

Red blood cells: This is where the color of our blood comes from. There are approximately 4-5 million red blood cells in a millimeter cube of blood. Their duty is to carry oxygen to cells that need it. Red blood cells perform their duty for about 100-120 days and then die. However, in order to regulate the number of red blood cells, our bodies produce 10,000 red blood cells a second.

White blood cells: There are approximately 4-10 thousand white blood cells in a millimeter cube of blood. These cells protect the body from microbes and viruses that enter the body. During an illness, their numbers increase from 10,000 up to 30,000 thousand per millimeter cube.

The two proteins are Fibrinogen and Thrombin. Fibrinogen is the potential clot material in the blood and Thrombin is the protein that initiates the process of blood clotting by slicing pieces out of Fibrinogen. In normal conditions blood clotting could be fatal. However, when there is an injury and a person is bleeding, blood clotting is essential to prevent death by bleeding. This is when these two proteins come into action. As soon as they receive the signal indicating to an injury, the Thrombin proteins begin to slice the Fibrinogen. The trimmed proteins are now called Fibrin. Fibrin proteins have sticky patches on their surfaces which allow them to stick to each other to form a net which in turn causes the blood clotting. Without a magnificent system such as this, we would all have bled to death.

So far, we have scrutinized only a millimeter cube of material from the human body and we are already amazed. Then imagine all the occurrences which take place in the entire body. We are not even aware of most of these miraculous mechanisms. Should we not stop to think of the designer, programmer and the implementer behind these fantastic organisms?

Can anyone claim that all of these occurrences are happening by means of randomness? If there is such a person, he should then amputate his own arm and wait to see if it grows back. Putting all of these arguments aside, not even the water that we drink could pour itself into a glass. Every event has a cause. Then what is the cause behind the magnificent system that exists in a millimeter cube of blood? To whom should we assign these incredible mechanisms? Systems that operate with knowledge, science, precision and know-how can only be assigned to an All-Knowing Being, Allah.

C. It is all nature's doing

What is nature? Everything we observe in our environment is considered as nature. We can say that all matter, great and small is a member of nature. Now, let us study one of these members, for example, the cow. A cow is not even aware of the milk it produces. What if we were to place a bucket of milk in front of a cow and ask it to turn it into yogurt? We must be all quite sure about this, it is impossible for a cow to turn milk into yogurt. How about if we invite all the rest of the members of nature to give a hand to the cow? If all the members of nature came together, they could not even create an atom, let alone a bucket of yogurt. Simply because all the components that form nature are a product of creation, hence they cannot create anything.

This means that Allah is the creator of everything. He exists and He is the One and only God. We are unable to see Him because we are being tested and assessed in this world. However, Allah has created many signs pointing to His existence, hence only those who possess intelligence are able to observe this. These signs are evident and present themselves on all matter from a tiny atom to immense galaxies and nebulas.

It is our duty to browse through the universe which resembles an art gallery displayed before our very eyes. Observing this splendid gallery will lead us to God. Thus, recognizing God will lead us to true love, the love of Allah.

In the holy Qur'an, Allah the Almighty states: "Everything in the seven heavens and on earth glorifies Him. There is nothing that does not praise Him with glorification..." (Qur'an, 7, 44) Most certainly, everything in the universe reflects His beauty and glorifies Him.

We shall now visit the grand art gallery of the universe and observe the beauty of Allah. Just like a honey bee, we will land on these masterpieces and collect information about their creator.

Everything is created with perfect measurements.

2. Universal harmony

Could we have survived if everything was not the way it is? For example, if rats were as big as camels or if horses were small as mice; what if we had some of the organs that animals have and vice versa? Imagine if one of our eyes was situated on our stomach and the other on our back. How about if our tongue was on our arm and if we had a nose like a Pelican? Can you imagine if our eyebrows kept on growing like our hair or if our teeth never stopped growing? To sum up, what if everything was different?

It is obvious that everything is created accordingly; hence all creatures receive what they essentially need.

The holy Qur'an asks, "Do they not see, how a camel is created?" So, let's follow the Qur'an's advice and take a look at a camel. A certain type of camel (Dromedary Camel) can survive without water for long periods of time. The secret is in the fat deposits preserved in its hump. When the animal faces dehydration, these fatty deposits break up, releasing hydrogen. The oxygen breathed in through the respiratory system is then mixed with hydrogen to produce water. Thanks to this miraculous biological system, in the desert environment camels can go without water for many days. If for example, a hundred chemists were to travel through the same desert without water, they would not be able to produce a single drop of water using the system that camels do. Then again, assuming that the camel produces this water using its intelligence would be quite absurd. Have you ever noticed how long a camel's eyelashes are? They are designed this way in order to protect their eyes from desert sandstorms. Another interesting thing about the camel is its lips. They are designed in such a perfect way that the upper lip is broken up in the middle so that the animal has no difficulty when it consumes prickly plants. The area of their feet is also quite large, and this is to protect them from being stuck in the soft sand. As you see, there are no coincidences in the camel's anatomy. We could easily say that everything was created to perfection.

3. Delicate balance in nature

Allah protects the delicate balance in nature by implementing an ecological equilibrium. This is done by the great food chain, which functions by animals eating plants and each other to protect the balance.

For example, a Praying Mantis is an insect about 8 cm long. It consumes insects that are considered as pests. The Praying Mantis contributes to the protection of the ecological balance by laying approximately 350 eggs at one time.

There is a type of rat which reproduces 400 young a year. According to a research the population growth from a one rat could reach 65,000 in two years. If the population growth of these species was not controlled by a divine balance, in a short time of two years the world would be covered by these species of rats.

There is also an amazing balance in the oceans. If there were no predators which fed on fish that lay millions of eggs at a time, then the oceans would be filled with fish. A type of fish called Haddock lays 6 million eggs a year.

Let us stay with the oceans. Did you know that every second, 16 million tons of water is converted to vapor on earth? This vapor is then distributed all over the world. If we wanted to simulate the heat energy needed to achieve this conversion, we would have to burn 410 trillion tons of coal per second. Thank God, 6,000 degrees of solar heat performs this automatically, saving us from an impossible task.

Let us analyze this vaporization process that occurs in the Mediterranean Sea. The Mediterranean Sea has an incredible climate. 116,000 tons of seawater is converted to water vapor every second. The water vapor then forms the clouds. Finally, these clouds ride the winds to carry rain water into those areas where it is needed. Now, simple logic says, how does the Mediterranean Sea compensate its losses? Calculations suggest that the Mediterranean Sea should lose a level of 1.5 meters a year. Once again, the divine program comes to the aid. The Mediterranean Sea also receives 31,000 tons of water per second. Some of it comes from the rivers that flow into it to provide 7,300 tons of water per second. There is still a deficit of 75,000 tons. This is provided by the Black Sea. The level of vaporization is quite low in the Black Sea, which is fed by three major rivers. Yet, this does not cause flooding because 6,000 tons of water per second is sent to the Mediterranean Sea. The remaining 70,000 tons of water is received from the Atlantic Ocean which flows into the Mediterranean through Gibraltar. The incredible balance in nature is quite evident even in our oceans.

4. Everything indicates to Him

The holy Qur'an states, *"Verily, all things We have created in proportion and measure"* (54, 49). From the tiniest matter to the largest objects, everything in the universe is created in proportion and precision. For example, the weight of a zygote (female egg cell) is 1.7 millionth of one gram. The process of dividing to produce the embryo and then transforming into a fully grown human being made up of 100 trillion living cells is quite delicate and is a function that follows precise measurements. Now let us ponder; is zygote intelligent enough to form each organ, designate their location with accuracy and assign duties upon them?

When we analyze only a single cell, we observe a chemical laboratory that has over 2,000 functions in progress. Human body is made up of approximately 100 trillion living cells. Within each cell there are chemical functions that take place with astonishing precision and perfect calculations. Most certainly, these functions do not occur by chance or coincidence. They are all part of a complex system implemented by a tremendous program.

The motion of planet earth is also controlled by precise measurements. The velocity of earth as it spins on its axis is significantly faster than the speed of sound. Had the earth spun faster, the gravitational pull would not have been sufficient enough to keep us on the surface. On the other hand, if earth rotated slower than its current speed, balance amongst the seasons would have been broken. Also vital to our survival is the distance between the earth and sun. This is approximately 150 million km. If we were closer or further away from the sun, life could not exist on earth. The best example of this is planet Venus and Mars. Venus having surface temperatures that melt down led; in contrast, the warmest place on Mars during daylight has a temperature of minus 22. These two planets are exceptional illustrations of how life conditions on earth could have been. The location of our Moon is also critical because of the affect it has on tides. In addition to these accurate measurements, our planet is tilted 23.5 degrees on its axis. This is quite significant as it plays an important role in the balance of oxygen and carbon dioxide. Certainly, all of these fantastic calculations point to a perfect Mathematician.

5. If God created everything, then who created God?

(We greatly regret the expression, but this is a question we frequently face)

Each time we hear this question, we should say, "O Muhammad, you are the truthful one!" The reason for this is, during the time of the Prophet, when people did not even imagine of asking such questions, the noble Prophet stated: "One day in the future, people will sit down with their legs crossed and ask, 'who created God?'"

Let us tackle this question with some analogies: Think about a train that has eighty wagons. If someone were to ask you, what pulls the last wagon, your answer would be, the wagon in front of it. If the questions continued in the same manner, you would keep on answering the same way, "the one in front of that one". However, when we reach the locomotive, this line of questioning would not make sense anymore. Simply, because the locomotive pulls all the wagons yet it does not need to be pulled, it is self-powered.

Now imagine that you are sitting on a chair that has no back legs. Obviously, you would fall back. However, in order to evade the fall, you have placed another chair underneath the one you are sitting on. Unfortunately, the second chair at the back also has its back legs missing. According to this analogy, you can line up a billion chairs at the back, and unless the very last chair has four legs you would still fall back. This means that we need a chair which supports everything but does not need support.

In the army a soldier receives his orders from his sergeant and the sergeant receives his orders from the captain. This chain of order goes all the way up to the general and the president of the country. It would be quite absurd to ask, "Where does the president receive his orders from?" Simply because, he would not be the president if he was receiving orders.

What we are trying to explain here is that in philosophy, one cannot enter into a debate of chain reaction; the reason for this is, if you were to argue that the creator was created by another being then the next question would be, "who created the being that created the creator". This line of questioning would never end unless you accept that there is one creator who does not need to be created. Of course, this creator is no other than Allah the Almighty, Who is the All-Powerful and Omnipotent. He creates all and He is the Eternal One.

As you see, the above examples clearly show that asking such a question is an act of ignorance.

There is an important question that we also face these days. In many chapters of the holy Qur'an when Allah refers to Himself, He uses the word, "We or Us". What is the divine reason behind this?

In some verses Allah uses the word "I" and in others He uses the word "We". One of the main reasons for this is the topic of the Verse. Let us analyze some verses from the holy Qur'an to get a better understanding of this:

> "O Children of Israel! Call to mind the (special) favour which I bestowed upon you, and fulfill your covenant with Me as I fulfill My Covenant with you, and fear none but Me" (Baqara, 40)

> "When My servants ask thee concerning Me, I am indeed close (to them): I listen to the prayer of every suppliant when he called on Me: Let them also, with a will, Listen to My call, and believe in Me: That they may walk in the right way." (Baqara, 186)

"*I have created the Jinn and Mankind only so that they may worship Me*" (Zariyat, 56) in verses such as the one's above Allah uses the pronoun "I". The reason for this is He is mentioning an issue which relates to His own Being. Hence, Allah does not permit any mediators in issues that concern His Being and Oneness.

However, when we analyze verses where the pronoun "We" is used, it becomes obvious that Allah is using this to explain about a servant which He uses as a mediator. For example, in the verses that describe the revelation of the Qur'an, "We have brought down the Qur'an" is used. This indicates to Archangel Gabriel (Jibril) through whom the holy Qur'an was revealed. Allah uses angels and other means not because He needs them but to display His infinite Power. We live in a world of cause and effect; therefore all occurrences were attached to a reason. For example, the mother and father is the reason attached to a baby's birth. However, sometimes Allah removes the reasons or causes such as in the case of Adam and the birth of Jesus (Isa). The power of Allah is not limited by causes. But, we live in a world of testing and assessment and this is why Allah creates a cause for everything. Let us take a look at some other examples in which the word "We" is used:

> *"We have, without doubt, sent down the Message; and We will assuredly guard it (from corruption)."* (Hijr, 9)

> *"Verily We shall give life to the dead, and We record that which they send before and that which they leave behind, and of all things have We taken account in a clear Book (of evidence)"* (Yasin, 12)

Even as human beings we frequently use the term "We" when we are referring to those under our command. For example, following a successful mission, an officer may use the following terminology, "We have done it".

6. How can we believe in things that we cannot see?

This is a question frequently asked by those who detach themselves from faith. There are many ways to tackle this question.

Belief is a quintessence of the heart. Believing in something can be achieved by using various paths. Seeing is only one of those many paths, however, it is not enough. For example, we cannot see sound, scent or taste. Physical pain or cold cannot be detected by the eye. The eye cannot reason or derive conclusions from occurrences. This is done by our intelligence. Now, if we consider the eye as the only tool of proving the existence of all entities, then the existence of properties such as sound, scent, flavor, feelings and thoughts should be rejected. So, instead of contradicting logic by renouncing the existence of these properties, we should acknowledge the fact that the eye alone is not enough to understand the existence.

Metaphysical entities which exist beyond the limits of our vision can only be detected with intelligence and absorbed by the heart. Even if we fail to understand with our mind, we confirm it with our heart. The reason for this is that even our logic and ration is limited. Therefore, we should recognize the limit of our intelligence and use our faith to reach beyond the boundaries of logic.

For example, during winter when we see traces of footsteps on snow, we quickly realize that a person has walked through there. If we investigate the size, depth and the shape of the footsteps, perhaps we might get some understanding regarding the person who left the marks. What this means is, we can obtain information about things we have not seen, by using things we observe. If we took a cow to the location where we had found the footsteps and asked the cow to give us some information, we would wait an eternity and not get an answer. Just because the cow has eyes, does not mean it understands. This proves that those who deny the existence of certain things simply because they cannot see them are no different to a cow.

7. The tree of Faith

We call upon those who have not received their share of this world, those who live in poverty as they were pushed aside by others.

We call upon those who were forgotten by others...those whose names are not mentioned in high society and those who are at the brink of starvation and dehydration...

Yes, we call upon all those who are in despair and hardship, whose hopes and expectations have faded away...those turned away from every door they had knocked and those who have no choice but to live on the streets.

Do not rebel because of your situation. Do not say:

– Allah made me poor by taking my world away. I have been abandoned by God. He has never helped me with anything. God did not give me wealth or reputation in this world. I have no value in the community. Yet everyone around me lives in prosperity and riches. I am a Muslim too...I also come from Adam and Eve. Then why do I suffer when others live in comfort?

O brother! These kinds of words should never come out of your mouth. You should examine your situation: First of all, there must be a divine reason for the current situation you are in. You were created as a free human being. Allah bestowed upon you such great gifts as patience, contentment and endurance. But at the same time, He has also given you beautiful gifts such as knowledge, faith and unity. The tree of faith which you possess has not decayed. It bears fresh seeds and saplings. Each day it grows stronger, producing new leaves. It is giving fruits. You do not need to protect it with sticks and stones.

The bounties Allah has given you in this world are small but enough to provide satisfaction. But do not forget that in the everlasting life, He has prepared for you bounties that no eye has beheld and no imagination could grasp. There, you shall receive these bounties in abundance. This is verified by a verse from the holy Qur'an: *"No soul is aware of what has been prepared in the hereafter. However, they are all bounties that provide great joy. They are rewards for deeds."*

This can be interpreted as: Those who follow His commandments in obedience will abstain from evil. They will submit to Allah, trusting Him with everything. In return, this behavior earns them great rewards in the life after.

8. Faith of a handicapped child

I couldn't take my eyes off him. He was only a child struggling to walk right in front of me. I could see that there was no feeling below his waste. He was having a hard time using the crutches. He couldn't have been older than thirteen. it was quite obvious that his efforts to walk had further shrunk his tiny body. I followed him as if I had been hypnotized. Suddenly, one of the crutches caught the sidewalk causing him to lose his balance. He fell to the ground. I ran towards him and attempted to lift him up. He was crying silently. I tried to comfort him by stroking his head:

– Do not worry... these things happen all the time.

– I am not worried. I am not even sad, he replied.

– But you are crying, I answered as I wiped his tears off.

– My arm hurts, this is why I wept.

I rolled his sleeves to see his injury, O my God! His left arm was amputated. This is why one of the crutches was designed specifically for that particular hand. He noticed my reaction as I stared at his prosthetic hand and said:

– This fall was nothing compared to my previous fall. That time a car ran over my hand.

I was lost for words, I did not know what else to say, hence I said:

– At least you are alive...

– It is ok... I am not sad or depressed. And i never complain about my condition, he replied.

– You said the same thing just before. What is the reason for this, I asked.

As he struggled to stand up with his puny arms, he replied:

– I believe in Allah. Those who believe will most certainly be given a strong healthy body in the everlasting life.

O my God! What was I hearing? I had never witnessed such great faith carried by such a small heart. Now, I was trembling more than him. He thanked me and slowly walked away. As I watched the little brave soul move, I thought "Who is more content, him or I?"

9. Taking advice

When the noble Prophet said, 'religion is advice' he was emphasizing an important principle in understanding the religion. It is essential for believers to seek knowledge with sincerity in order recognize the Creator. There are those who listen to the truth brought by the Messenger of Allah, yet they do not absorb it.

Consequently, they fail to benefit from divine mercy. There are others who listen and understand, but fail to act upon their knowledge. They do not realize that Allah would make things easier according to their intentions. On the other hand, there are also those who listen, understand and practice all they have learned with sincerity. These are the servants with whom Allah is pleased.

Yes, one must show great passion towards learning the issues regarding life after death. The sensitivity displayed towards the issue also indicates to respect towards Allah. We must never forget that this is the only way to attain a palace in Paradise.

10. Benefiting from Divine Mercy

Humans were created as rational beings with the ability of deriving a lesson from each event and experience they encounter in life. Using this ability, we can analyze the lives of those brave souls of history and predict what lies ahead for us and for our friends. We are indeed transient beings and just as the human race, all of God's creation is transient. However, although mankind is transient in this life, he will live for eternity in the next. Initially these good tidings were brought to us by the Prophet, continued by the scholars who brighten our world with the light they obtained from him. Since, this is the reality and our world is transitory; and since there is a life of eternity with two possible endings, Heaven or Hell, then it should be our most important priority to succeed in obtaining an everlasting life in Paradise. This means that it is imperative for us to learn our religion. And during the learning process, we need to concentrate on the following points:

We must encourage ourselves to comprehend the subject. We must not let Satan deceive us with his trickery. A person should always keep his mind and heart open to good advice. An intention to learn is the most important issue because Allah guides people according to their intentions. Listening with sincerity and intention to learn was the greatest distinction between Abu-Bakr who was fortunate enough to learn from the Prophet himself and Abu Jahl, who was the father of ignorance. During the lessons, whenever we hear the words arrogance, hypocrisy and suspicion, we should always take it upon us to question our own carnal soul, "Do I have such a character?" One should always question his own behavior.

Also during a lesson, if the name of a Companion or a great scholar is mentioned, we should ask ourselves, "Could I have shown the same righteousness if I was in his shoes?"

All believers should display great sensitivity towards the issues mentioned above and constantly pray to Allah for His aid in finding the right path.

11. The owner of the word

It is imperative that we take notice of all cautions put forward to us, in order to succeed in life and also to avoid making mistakes. Whether they are young or old, we should at least respect the views of those who wish to offer their advice to us. In any case we should not prejudge anyone. However, one should never forget that the best indication to an advisor's character is his lifestyle and behavior. This is the way we can decide whether a person is worthy of giving advice. For example, if a doctor, who is a smoker, gave you advice regarding the harm that cigarettes cause to your health, to what extent would he/she be affective? If you were intending to establish a business, would you take advice from a businessman who has been bankrupt over and over again? No matter, which branch we are interested in, whether it is political science, social issues or religion, it is important to be choosy when it comes to seeking advice.

For example, it was the advice taken from the cursed Satan to eat the fruit of the forbidden tree which caused the extradition of Adam and Eve from Paradise. Do not forget that an evil man such as Abu Jahl also attempted to give advice to those who had listened to recommendations of the noble Prophet. This is why it is very important to analyze those who wish to give advice to us. When religion is in concern, we should first look to see if the person is practicing what he preaches. The reason for this is, Satan gives the most advice in the name of religion but his intentions are to sway those who listen to him, away from the path of Allah.

In conclusion, one must be extremely careful on taking advice regarding religious matters, and should lean only towards those who seek to please Allah. isn't it a fact that many people ruin their lives because of their choices?

CHAPTER FOUR

1. Young person

Have you thought about existence, beginning from a tiny molecule to distances beyond your imagination? Take a look at your own anatomy; can you discriminate between your organs or prefer one organ over another? Young man, in an era where science and technology have reached dizzy heights, one of the greatest doctor's of our time states, "O magnificent organ! In total respect, I bow in front of you!" He was referring to our nose. Why was he so captivated with this organ?

Wouldn't you like to recognize yourself through knowledge? If you insist on running away from yourself, one day your own organs will stand on your path with their delicate design and anatomy.

Will you still refrain from scrutinizing the minute details of your own body which is formed by such perfect components? You intend to conquer the world yet you still insist on remaining as a stranger to your own religion.

Will you not stop to think about your own magnificent being? Have you ever thought what would happen if you changed the location of your organs or removed them completely?

You are a being made to think. Hence your thoughts will lead you to new discoveries through which you shall establish new worlds. Isn't it time that you thought and discovered yourself?

2. Tito's historical confessions

Salih Gökkaya was a man who had spent 50 years of his life promoting the ideology of Communism. He became quite famous through his struggle for this false cause. Fortunately, in the late years of his life, he discovered Islam. He died as a man honored by Islam. However, during the times when he was a radical Communist, he was invited to Yugoslavia. Those days, he held the title of 'President of Turkish Communist Student Organization'. in his visit to Belgrade, he met Admiral Tito.

Tito was an old man who had sacrificed his life for Communism. His confessions of regret in his grand old age were quite interesting:

– Comrades, I am dying …and I cannot describe the horridness of death to you. Even if I was capable of this, you would not comprehend the seriousness of death because you are still young. Just imagine your dead…and do not exist anymore. Once you enter the grave, you are gone, never to return again. This is driving me crazy. Being separated from loved ones, friends and possessions and leaving this world never to behold its beauty again. Do you understand what this means? Dear comrades, I want to tell you something with all my sincerity. When I die, if my body is going to decompose into the earth, if there is no resurrection and no reward or punishment, then what is the meaning of our efforts? Tell me comrades, after I die, what benefit will I have if I lived in the hearts of people and was never forgotten. Will the praises and applauses of people save my decomposing body?

Tell me where we are going? Lenin, Marks or Mao has not provided any answers to these questions. I have to confess, that I now believe in God, His Prophets and in the life after death. Atheism is not the solution. Just think about it for a moment, this universe has to have a creator and an implementer of laws. I believe death is not the end.

There must be a place of justice where those who died innocently and tyrants who die without punishment are judged. There is no true justice in this world…this is not real, such chaos cannot exist. I feel this in my conscience. All the wrongs we have done to millions of people are now eating me away. Someone must hear their screams for justice…how else can there be reconciliation? Carl Marx has failed us in this issue, we have been brainwashed.

For some reason we do not realize this until death knocks on our doors. Sometimes we are deceived by our thrones and high positions. These are my views comrades; you make up your own minds.

3. Sir Isaac Newton

Isaac Newton is regarded as one of the greatest physicist of all times. He earned this honor through his work with mathematical integers, differentials, laws of motion and of course his most famous calculations of the universal gravitational constant that establishes a connection between an apple falling from a tree to planets, stars and galaxies.

Isaac Newton was born in 1642 in England. It was the same year his predecessor Galileo had died. His life is decorated with achievements, accomplishments, triumphs and success. Unlike Galileo, his fate was not full of despair, misery and disappointment. Bernard Russell states: "The only thing that would even come close to the beautiful works produced by Newton is Albert Einstein's theory of relativity".

There is no doubt that the universe could be viewed from many aspects such as mechanical, physical, esthetic, philosophical and physiological. Of course a genius such as Newton couldn't have neglected any of them.

In his famous work, Principia, he states, "The harmonious system observed in the sun, planets and comets can only be the work of a Powerful Being who is the All-knowing. God is eternal and He is present everywhere and He is the All-seeing." A few years back, there was an article published in the Minnesota Technology:

"Once, Isaac Newton had constructed a mechanical model of the solar system. The model was operated by a mechanical arm. As the lever was turned the planets began to rotate around the model sun with their corresponding systems. One day, an associate of Newton who did not believe in God came to his house. He was astounded by Newton's model of the solar system. Curiously, he asked:

– This is beautiful. Who made this?

– No one did, replied Newton.

– Perhaps you did not understand my question.

– I most certainly did. This model is a product of chance. It eventually evolved into its current condition, said Newton.

– Do you think that I am a fool?

At this point Newton stood up, and then placing his hand on his guest's shoulder, he replied:

– This mechanism you see is only a simple model of the real solar system which operates with astonishing principles and laws. You are arguing that even such a basic model has to have a maker, yet you still refuse to recognize the creator of the real thing?

In the 28th question of his book titled Optics, Newton states: "The priority of natural philosophy (Physics) is to bring proofs to events without getting caught in hypothesis and to discover the initial non-mechanical cause working backwards from the effects." "Can we not then, find the All-knowing, All-powerful, All-seeing eternal God through physical occurrences?" "Indeed, God is not just an initial cause who established the mechanism of the universe and then left it to work by itself. He possesses the power to control all events, past, current and future. He knows with His eternal knowledge and governs with His Might."

Newton did not restrict himself to long mathematical formulas and calculations; he has proven the existence of God by pointing out the harmony, order and reason that is evident in the universe. His ideology, "Everything happens for a reason" was based on magnificent occurrences in nature, such as the perfect laws which govern the motions of heavenly bodies, the beauty and order observed in the universe and incredible tasks performed by animals. Through physics and mathematics, Newton has shown that all of these astounding occurrences are done by the power of God.

Let us continue with Newton's thoughts: How did the organs of animals form in such a superb way? Is it possible to make an eye without knowledge in optical science? Can an ear be constructed without knowledge in acoustics, noise or vibration? Where do animals learn to behave in such amazing manner? There is no doubt about the existence of a Creator. The complexity even in the smallest matter, with its tiny components designed in perfect harmony with space and time insists on a Being whose knowledge is infinite.

4. Evidence of God's existence

A man came to William Paley and said, "There is no God, can you prove me wrong?" Paley reached into his pocket and took out a watch. Then opening its cover, he said: "If I argued that all of these tiny complex components, such as springs and wheels came together by a coincidence to form this watch and then continued to work in harmony by chance; wouldn't you doubt my sanity? Then, I urge you to observe the heavens and take a good look how all stars and planets follow a particular path and motion.

The earth and the rest of the planets are in perfect motion and follow a precise route of rotation around the sun. At the same time our solar system is orbiting the Milky Way galaxy, traveling at a velocity of 250 km/sec. This means that it takes 250 million years to revolve once around the Milky Way. There are approximately 200 billion stars in our galaxy and just as our sun, they are all in motion. It is quite fascinating to think that they all move harmoniously with tremendous speeds. There is no room for chaos in the universe. Now, which is easier to believe? Everything appeared by chance or everything is created by God and He is the one that keeps it all in order.

5. A million proofs

Islam is a complete religion. This means that one cannot take certain parts out of it and still claim to believe. Yes, Islam is a religion of guidance and with its obligatory acts and prohibitions it shows humanity how to achieve happiness in both worlds. Beginning with Prophet Muhammad, peace and blessings be upon him, all great scholars and clerics have explained the beauty of Islam in a manner which convinces the mind and satisfies the heart. However, we must understand that religion cannot be comprehended with intelligence and logic alone. If that was the case, then it would not be regarded as faith; instead it would have been a discipline in science. Sometimes, people have difficulties in comprehending certain issues of religion. There are two reasons for this; one is the lack of research. It is important to find the correct publications that provide answers to our questions. The second reason is, sometimes we try to comprehend matters that cannot be grasped with the mind. For example, it is impossible to comprehend the infinite knowledge of God, using our limited minds.

Also, Satan uses a tiny sign of doubt to refute hundreds of proofs regarding the reality of faith. Whereas, it is a clear fact that the testimony of one witness is preferred over a hundred non-witnesses. Here is an example:

Imagine a palace that has hundreds of doors. And let us say that many of these doors provide access to the palace. Can anyone who stands in front of one locked door, claim that it is impossible to enter this palace?

Just as the example, the reality of faith is like a palace which has hundreds of doors through which you can enter. It cannot be denied by one closed door. However, Satan points to the closed door, taking one's attention away from the hundreds of entrances that stand before their very eyes. He whispers cunningly, "There is no way into this palace, perhaps it is not even a palace".

6. A blind man

A blind man was begging on the street when another man accidentally ran into him. Then with rage he shouted, "Ok I couldn't see you but why don't you at least look where you're going... Are you blind!"

In shock, the blind beggar replied, "Are you blind as well?" The other man answered, "Yes I am...how ironic a blind man running into another blind man. Perhaps you are the only person that would understand me".

The two men sat down for awhile and had a heart to heart. During the conversation, the blind beggar asked the other man how much he earned a day. The other man said, "A fair amount" as he took his money bag out. The blind beggar quickly grabbed the bag full of money and walked away, thinking that the other man could not catch him, since he was also blind. However, as he attempted to make a getaway, he felt a rock hitting him behind the head. For a brief second, he wobbled but once again tried to walk away. Suddenly, another rock smashed into his back, followed by another and then another. They were all finding their target. Finally, the blind beggar stopped and shouted:

"What is going on here my friend. I do not think a blind man could cast stones like that!"

The moral of the story is that stones cast by a blind man cannot consistently find their target by chance. If they did, we have to agree that the person throwing the rocks is not blind. Now, keeping in mind the analogy above, let us think about the universe and the billions of stars, galaxies, planets and other heavenly bodies moving in perfect motion and harmony for billions of years. Is there any possibility of a **blind chance** being involved in such a beautiful order and harmony?

Let us take a look at the following examples:

a) If the crust of the earth was a few meters thicker than its current size, all oxygen would have been absorbed by carbon-dioxide; hence organic life couldn't have existed on earth.

b) If the atmosphere had been thinner than it is now, cosmic rays, meteors, and other space objects entering through the atmosphere would have destroyed life on earth.

c) If the moon was 30 km closer to earth, the high tides would have covered all land on earth with water.

d) If the oceans were made up of sweet water, we could not have endured the putrefying odor. Salt stops the oceans from turning into giant swamps hence if sodium and chloride had not bonded, life could not have existed.

e) Without the bonding of chemical elements there would be no earth, water, trees, animals or plants.

We cannot accept that even a simple picture or a table could form by a coincidence, then how could anyone believe in a story which claims that all natural occurrences are coincidental and random.

7. Lying

In a verse, Allah the Almighty describes the servants of the All-Merciful: *"Those who witness no falsehood, and, if they pass by futility, they pass by it with honorable (avoidance)."* (Qur'an, 25/72) This means that the true servants of the All-merciful do not lie or even come close it. There is a similar indication in a verse regarding Ramadan, "Whoever, sees the face of Ramadan...does not bear false witness".

The priority interpretation of this verse is, 'the servants of the All-Merciful do not even come face to face with a lie'. Exaggeration or talking non-sense is also considered as lying.

In this day and age, the people of the east in particular have been victimized by lies. This appalling illness is also creeping into western societies. Lying is a serious problem, a human weakness which threatens peace, harmony and security of the people of the world. At first, a small lie might seem as quite harmless and insignificant. However, soon it becomes the biggest sin of all major sins.

Although lying comes third in the list of major sins mentioned above, each time the subject of lying arose, the noble Prophet said, "Do not incline towards lying". Why is it so important to refrain from lies? There is a lie at the root of all evil deeds. Assigning partners to Allah and rebellion to parents are also a type of lie. If you analyzed the reason of lying, you will realize that all sins flourish from the soil of lies. This is why the noble Prophet insisted on advising people to refrain from lying. Assigning partners to God is the biggest lie. Take a look at your daily lives and scrutinize the events that occur around you. Every lie is told in the name of a false god. Human beings do not need to lie in order to survive.

It is natural for a human being to speak the truth. This means that we are created in such nature that it continuously persuades us to tell the truth. The amount of lies a person tells in a day, indicates to the amount of false gods which he worships. The reason for this is a lie is told with an intention of submission to a false god. For example, a person may resort to lies in order to conceal his faults. By doing so, he is turning his back on the truth to achieve his goal by deceiving those around him.

There is also an objective in worshiping Allah. It is to obtain all the beautiful bounties of life through worship. However, those who have broken all ties with Allah try to obtain this through lies. They use lies to reach their target. Eventually, this terrible habit becomes a part of their lives. Consequently, lies begin to crawl around in politics and business affairs. Relationships between mothers, fathers, partners and children begin to revolve around lies. Friendships transform into a big lie. Finally, life loses its meaning becoming a device of hypocrisy. People then begin to worship lies unaware of the fact that they have turned into a polytheist. As a result, they die and go to Allah as polytheists.

We must never forget the fact that no one lies unless they have a personal gain from it. Secondly, every lie is an act of hypocrisy. This is a tool that measures one's faith in the One and only God. One's sincerity in faith can be measured by his choice between lie and truth.

However, there are exceptions. Some people are compulsive liars. It is like sickness, because they lie without a reason. Therefore, we cannot claim that they worship a lie that has an objective. For example, prayers become so much a habit with some people that they are not even aware of why they pray. Yet sometimes, prayers are performed in total awareness. This is the true form of worship. A habitual prayer is acceptable, because an obligation has been completed however it lacks the true soul of an authentic worship. This analogy also describes the seriousness of lying. When a person lies in total awareness, he is worshipping false gods. Although all lies are a form of hypocrisy, those that lie in total unawareness should be excluded.

The holy Qur'an clarifies the issue with the following verse, "Allah will hold you responsible for the oaths you have taken, accept for those false promises (pointless) you make". This is a great blessing from God. He knows that sometimes we make habitual promises even though we know that they will not be kept.

However, our noble Prophet says that even pointless lies (such as lies used in jokes) carry great risks. The risks associated with them are that they will eventually become a habit and drag their holder into Hellfire.

Abdullah Ibn Masud narrates: "The messenger of Allah said, "Be truthful because truth will take you to good, and good will take you into paradise. A person speaks the truth and makes the effort to be honest. Then one day, he will be given the title of 'Siddiq', by the side of Allah."

This is an important sentence, "One tries to be honest by speaking the truth", followed by "And Allah gives them the title of Siddiq". The noble Messenger gives us the good news through this Hadith. It is not that easy to purify oneself from all lies in one go. However, those who intend to tell the truth at all times and display a sincere effort towards honesty will eventually be rewarded. Hence, one day, they shall be known as honest by the side of Allah.

The above Hadith continues as, "Abstain from lying, because lies will take you to sins and sins will take you to Hell.

Now let us think dear friends, what the holy Qur'an, Hadith and the noble Prophet says about lying. Do you think we could still tell a lie?

CHAPTER FIVE

First word

B*ismillah,* In the Name of God, is the start of all things good. We too shall start with it. Know, O my soul! Just as this blessed phrase is a mark of Islam, so too, it is constantly recited by all beings through their tongues of disposition. If you want to know what an inexhaustible strength, what an unending source of bounty is *Bismillah,* listen to the following story which is in the form of a comparison. It goes like this:

Someone who makes a journey through the deserts of Arabia has to travel in the name of a tribal chief and enter under his protection, for in this way he may be saved from the assaults of bandits and secure his needs. On his own he will perish in the face of innumerable enemies and needs. And so, two men went on such a journey and entered the desert. One of them was modest and humble, the other proud and conceited. The humble man assumed the name of a tribal chief, while the proud man did not. The first travelled safely wherever he went. If he encountered bandits, he said: "I am travelling in the name of such-and-such tribal leader," and they would not molest him. If he came to some tents, he would be treated respectfully due to the name. But the proud man suffered such calamities throughout his journey that they cannot be described. He both trembled before everything and begged from everything. He was abased and became an object of scorn.

And so, my proud soul! You are the traveler, and this world is a desert. Your impotence and poverty have no limit, and your enemies and needs are endless. Since it is thus, take the name of the Pre-Eternal Ruler and Post-Eternal Lord of the desert and be saved from begging before the whole universe and trembling before every event.

Indeed, this phrase is a treasury so blessed that your infinite impotence and want bind you to an infinite power and mercy; it makes that impotence and want a most acceptable intercessor at the Court of One All-Powerful and Compassionate. The person who acts saying, "In the Name of God," resembles someone who enrolls in the army. He acts in the name of the government; he has fear of no one; he speaks, performs every matter, and withstands everything in the name of the law and the name of the government.

At the beginning we said that all beings say, "In the Name of God" through the tongue of disposition. Is that so?

Indeed, it is so. If you were to see that a single person had come and had driven all the inhabitants of a town to a place by force and compelled them to work, you would be certain that he had not acted in his own name and through his own power, but that he was a soldier, acting in the name of the government and relying on the power of a king.

In the same way, all things act in the name of Almighty God, for minute things like seeds and grains bear huge trees on their heads; they raise loads like mountains. That means all trees say: "In the Name of God," fill their hands from the treasury of Mercy, and offer them to us. All gardens say: "In the Name of God," and become cauldrons from the kitchens of Divine Power in which are cooked numerous varieties of different foods. All blessed animals like cows, camels, sheep, and goats, say: "In the Name of God," and become fountains of milk from the abundance of Mercy, offering us a most delicate and pure food like the water of life in the name of the Provider. The roots and rootlets, soft as silk, of all plants, trees, and grasses, say: "In the Name of God," and pierce and pass through hard rock and earth. Mentioning the name of God, the name of the Most Merciful, everything becomes subjected to them."""

Indeed, the roots spreading through hard rock and earth and producing fruits as easily as the branches spread through the air and produce fruits, and the delicate green leaves retaining their moisture for months in the face of extreme heat, deal a slap in the mouths of Naturalists and jab a finger in their blind eyes, saying: "Even heat and hardness, in which you most trust, are under a command. For, like the Staff of Moses, each of those silken rootlets conform to the command of, *And We said, O Moses, strike the rock with your staff,* and split the rock. And the delicate leaves fine as cigarette paper recite the verse, *O fire be coolness and peace* against the heat of the fire, each like the members of Abraham (UWP).

Since all things say, "In the Name of God," and bearing God's bounties in God's name, give them to us, we too should say, "In the Name of God." We should give in the name of God, and take in the name of God. And we should not take from heedless people who neglect to give in God's name.

Question: We give a price to people, who are like tray-bearers. So what price does God the true owner want?

The Answer: Yes, the price the True Bestower of Bounties wants in return for those valuable bounties and goods is three things: one is **remembrance,** one is **thanks,** and one is **reflection.** Saying, "In the Name of God" at the start is remembrance, and, "All praise be to God" at the end is thanks. And perceiving and thinking of those bounties, which are valuable wonders of art, being miracles of power of the Unique and Eternally Besought One and gifts of His mercy, is reflection. However foolish it is to kiss the foot of a lowly man who conveys to you the valuable gift of a king and not to recognize the gift's owner, to praise and love the apparent source of bounties and forget the True Bestower of Bounties is a thousand times more foolish.

O my soul! If you do not wish to be foolish in that way, give in God's name, take in God's name, begin in God's name, and act in God's name.

Second word

In the Name of God, the Merciful, the Compassionate. Those who believe in the Unseen.

If you want to understand what great happiness and bounty, what great pleasure and ease is to be found in belief in God, listen to this story which is in the form of a comparison:

One time, two men went on a journey for both pleasure and business. One set off in a selfish, inauspicious direction; the other on a godly, propitious way.

Since the selfish man was both conceited, self-centered, and pessimistic, he ended up in what seemed to him to be a most wicked country due to his pessimism. He looked around and everywhere saw the powerless and the unfortunate lamenting in the grasp and at the destruction of fearsome bullying tyrants. He saw the same grievous, painful situation in all the places he travelled. The whole country took on the form of a house of mourning. Apart from becoming drunk, he could find no way of not noticing this grievous and somber situation. For everyone seemed to him to be an enemy and foreign. And all around he saw horrible corpses and despairing, weeping orphans. His conscience was in a state of torment.

The other man was godly, devout, fair-minded, and with fine morals so that the country he came to was most excellent in his view. This good man saw universal rejoicing in the land he had entered. Everywhere was a joyful festival, a place for the remembrance of God overflowing with rapture and happiness; everyone seemed to him a friend and relation. Throughout the country he saw the festive celebrations of a general discharge from duties accompanied by cries of good wishes and thanks. And he also heard the sound of a drum and band for the enlistment of soldiers with happy calls of "God is Most Great!" and "There is no god but God!" Rather than being grieved at the suffering of both himself and all the people like the first miserable man, this fortunate man was pleased and happy at both his own joy and that of all the inhabitants. Furthermore, he was able to do some profitable trade. He offered thanks to God.

After some while he returned and came across the other man. He understood his condition, and said to him: "You were out of your mind. The ugliness inside you must have been reflected on the outer world so that you imagined laughter to be weeping, and the discharge from duties to be sack and pillage. Come to your senses and purify your heart so that this calamitous veil is raised from your eyes and you can see the truth.

For the country of an utterly just, compassionate, beneficent, powerful, order-loving, and kind king could not be in the way you imagined, nor could a country which demonstrated this number of clear signs of progress and achievement." The unhappy man later came to his senses and repented. He said, "Yes, I was crazy through drink. May God be pleased with you, you have saved me from a hellish state."

O my soul! Know that the first man represents an unbeliever, or someone depraved and heedless. In his view the world is a house of universal mourning. All living creature are orphans weeping at the blows of death and separation. Man and the animals are alone and without ties being ripped apart by the talons of the appointed hour. Mighty beings like the mountains and oceans are like horrendous, lifeless corpses. Many grievous, crushing, terrifying delusions like these arise from his unbelief and misguidance, and torment him.

As for the other man, he is a believer. He recognizes and affirms Almighty God. In his view this world is an abode where the Name of the All-Merciful One is constantly recited, a place of instruction for man and the animals, and a field of examination for man and jinn. All animal and human deaths are demobilization. Those who have completed their duties of life depart from this transient world for another, happy and trouble-free, world so that place may be made for new officials to come and work. The birth of all animals and humans forms their enlistment into the army, their being taken under arms, and the start of their duties. Each living being is a joyful regular soldier, an honest, contented official. And all voices, both glorification of God and the recitation of His Names at the outset of their duties, and the thanks and rejoicing at their ceasing work, or the songs arising from their joy at working. In the view of the believer, all beings are the friendly servants, amicable officials, and agreeable books of his Most Generous Lord and All-Compassionate Owner. Very many more subtle, exalted, pleasurable, and sweet truths like these become manifest and appear from his belief.

That is to say, belief in God bears the seed of what is in effect a Tuba Tree of Paradise, while unbelief conceals the seed of a Zakkum Tree of Hell.

That means that safety and security are only to be found in Islam and belief. In which case, we should continually say, "Praise be to God for the religion of Islam and perfect belief."

1. Thoughts on vehicles

These days, cars play a great role in our daily lives especially with the great population growth in the cities of the world. There are many types of vehicles, with fast sports cars and luxurious automobiles taking the top spots in the favorite list. Obviously, every car has a designer and an engineer. However, when you look at the issue from an engineer's point of view and the consumers, you will see that there are many different people involved in the construction of a vehicle. For example, the head lights of a vehicle remind you of Edison. If he had not invented the light globe, there would be no head lights. Considering that this is only a small component in a complex system. What about the tires made from petroleum? The invention of plastic must have been a difficult process. How about the windows? Many people must have endured hard work and long hours to come up with such technology. An engineer who built cars does not bother with these inventions. He chooses the ones he needs and adapts them into his own design. What is really interesting is the fact that the applications performed by the engineer is intelligent and corresponds to our needs. The wheels are round because it is the most suitable shape for the road. There are powerful head lights at the front of the vehicle because the driver needs them at night. The vehicles are fitted with horns, so that other drivers or pedestrians can be warned when necessary. Vehicles are also fitted with heaters so that people could keep warm during winter. Even the safety of drivers and passengers is assured with seat belts.

Yes, we can add many more examples regarding the design of vehicles. In summary, it is quite obvious that an engineer possesses knowledge about many inventions, consumer needs and the conditions in the environment.

Now, let us think about the mechanical system of the human body. It needs energy to survive. Human beings obtain this energy from plants and animals in the environment, just like a vehicle that visits a petrol station when it's low on fuel. With human beings, breathing is one of the most imperative processes of life. The atmosphere contains the exact mixture of oxygen and other gases vital for human lungs. The great biological engineer is aware of this composition hence he has adjusted the firing system of the engine accordingly. Water is another vital substance for our survival. Our bodies need water. It also cools us down and helps the digestive system. And again the great designer uses water to cool the engine down, because he is aware of this quality of water.

All the comparisons above constitute only one part of our topic. How about our tongues? Someone who has no knowledge of human taste buds or the ingredients of fruits and vegetables cannot create a human being. Once again, someone that has no knowledge about thousands of flowers and the pollen they produce cannot create the honeybee. It is in human nature to value himself over anyone else, however, with the compassion miraculously placed in his/her heart, parents become servants of their young. The technology we observe in motor vehicles is an indication of engineer's knowledge. Just as the example, the composition of water, which is vital for the survival of all living beings, the precise positioning of the sun and its ultra-violet rays, also essential for our survival, indicates to an All-Knowing engineer. This means that there is a relation between all matter in the universe and this in turn points to one governing hand.

2. Those that brightened the middle ages

Emperor Charlemagne (742-814) was the most famous king of the middle ages. He did not even know how to write. His efforts to seek knowledge had failed. Those days, the Eastern Roman Empire, based in Istanbul was no different. Education was limited to writings of Aristotle and other ancient books. The only positive development would be the efforts of Leon the VI to teach mathematics in 911AD. At the same era, Harun Rashed (763-809) was the protector of science and knowledge. The famous alarm clock he sent to Charlemagne as a gift is an exceptional fact of history.

In an age when humanity lived in ignorance, Islamic civilizations had rapidly developed due their hunger for knowledge. They made significant progress in the fields of science, astronomy, mathematics and geography.

During the time of Caliph Al-Ma'mun (786-833) a huge library by the name of 'Bayt'ul Hikma' (house of wisdom) and an observatory was established in Baghdad. Vast astronomical researches were conducted regarding the inclination of the earth and the sun. The 23 degree inclination of the earth was discovered. Charts describing the motions of planets were drawn and a map of the world was prepared in Baghdad. The mathematicians of Baghdad had even calculated the length of the meridian as 123300 meters. They were only 2360 meters off from the modern data, which means the error margin was 2%. Their efforts had enabled many scientists to obtain information about the size of the earth.

The two of the most famous Islamic scientists who lived around 800AD proposed theories which counterpart the science of today.

Kindi was born in Kufa. In one of his writings he argues, "Space, time, matter and motion did not appear before or after each other. They are all part of one essential and were created at the same time. Just as matter, time also has an end, and all of these findings point to the existence of the Creator." It was the verses of the holy Qur'an that encouraged Kindi to seek knowledge from philosophy to physics. The Grand Unified Theory and Einstein's Theory of Relativity confirms his findings.

Over a thousand years ago during the time of Abbasids, Jabir Ibn Hayyan, a scholar of physics and chemistry taught in the Madrasa of Harran. In one of his lectures delivered to students arriving from many parts of the world, he stated: "Matter is dense energy. The argument of Greek physicists that claim matter is solid hence it can only be divided until the smallest particle, is wrong. Even the smallest particle (atom) can be divided and it will release energy. This energy is so immense, may Allah protect us, that it has the potential to destroy Baghdad.

Most certainly, the verse from the holy Qur'an stating that even the smallest particle is made up of smaller parts, encouraged the Turkish scientist Jabir Ibn Hayyan to become the father of quantum physics. The Madrasa of Harran provided education in mathematics, physics, chemistry and natural sciences. Jabir was given the title of "Chief Scholar', in today's terms 'University Chancellor' by Harun Rashed. He has written 826 books. 112 applied physics, 70 theoretical chemistry, 144 minerals and forces that cannot be explained by physics and chemistry and 500 books in theoretical physics, chemistry, astronomy, philosophy and history of religions.

Jabir also indicated that matter can change form by physical modification in their atomic values. He argued that metals could be converted to other metals if their atomic values were changed. Jabir also discovered physical laws regarding optics and established the theory of lens. He has used mirrors to obtain energy from the sun.

According to Western scientists, Jabir is one of the 12 scientific geniuses of all times. Jabir is also the inventor of algebra, which is appropriately named after him, Al-Jabir.

Another significant figure of the era is Omar Khayyam (1016-1123). He was a scholar, poet and a judge. The claims that some of his poetry contained anti-religious remarks are wrong. His original poetry is no more than 40 quatrains and none of them contain anti-religious implications.

His works include algebraic equations and solutions, cubic equations and fractions. Khayyam also provided the $n=2, 3, 4...$ which is quite similar to one of Newton's formulas. Khayyam also provided the formulas for triangular calculations. Today we use the term Pascal's triangle for this equation yet Khayyam lived 500 years before Pascal and Newton, hence the name for these two should really be, 'Khayyam's formula' and Khayyam's triangle'.

Omar Khayyam also provided formulas for finding square-roots and cubic-roots. His book regarding cubic equations consists of 52 pages. Khayyam was the first man to use algebra in geometric calculations. Omar Khayyam questioned Euclidean calculations and offered new theories regarding geometry. Later, his theories were taken up by Turkish mathematician Nasreddin al Tusi and then transferred to Western countries. Omar Khayyam also has books on astronomy.

History has witnessed many kings and emperors who supported and encouraged scientific research and education. However, there is only one emperor who was a scientist himself. It was the great Turkish emperor and astronomer, Ulugh Bey (1394-1449).

Ulugh Bey's astronomical table titled "Ziyc" is regarded as the second greatest star catalogue following the Almanac of Al-Batlamyus. The catalogue prepared by Ulugh Bey contained the locations of 1018 stars. It was completed in the year 1437, yet the Europeans got a hold of it 100 years later. It is said that out of all catalogues prepared until the 17th century, it is the most accurate one. Ulugh Bey's teacher, Kadizade Rumi is considered as the Plato of his era. With Iyaseddin Jamshid they established an observatory in Samarqand. In this observatory studies and observations were conducted on planets, Earth, Mercury, Venus, Mars, Jupiter, Saturn and Uranus. Remarkable calculations were recorded.

During the VII century there were 2 dozen hospitals established in Anatolia. About the same time, Sufi lodges were looking after spiritual health and investigating the cause of mental illnesses. In the XV century, Fatih Sultan Muhammad (1431-1481) began a university program in Istanbul (1453) studying medicine and geometry. Astronomical researches were increased during the period, after Fatih invited Ali Kuscu, a student of Ulugh Bey to Istanbul following the death of his teacher. Ali Kuscu became one of Fatih's scientists. He has modified many theories in astronomy and written a number of books.

In his four volumes of 'Introduction to the history of science', George Sarton designates hundreds of references to contributions made by Islamic scientists. The Middle-Ages were in abundance of Muslim scientists who have shown humanity a bright path to follow and the results of unifying the heart and intelligence. Although they lived a long time ago, their views are still valued and utilized by modern science. There is no doubt that the secret of this incredible success is the bond which they all had with the 'Source', (Qur'an).

3. Return to life

In this article we are faced with an actual event. An event that seems quite simple at first, yet it triggers a fundamental change. The fact is, a stone thrown at a herd of sheep that is about to run into hazardous territory causes a change in direction. The shepherd casts the stone to protect his herd. This is an important lesson for us because the stones of misfortune falling upon our heads are an indication of changes which we need to make in our lives. Now and then, we need to stop and think about what kind of path we are on. Is there a danger ahead? How should I change if I am on the wrong path? We need to question ourselves before the day of great questioning arrives. Now, let us listen to a person who wished to change his life:

When I regained consciousness, my body was aching all over and my head felt like it weighed a ton. I was lying on the ground in a tiny, dark place. As I tried to straighten myself, I hit my head on a piece of timber. My eyes were wide open but I could not see anything. My fear began to increase by the minute as I was drenched in sweat.

I thought of my life as I attempted to make a connection with the place I was in. Suddenly, the thought of death crossed my mind. The deadened feeling of fear quickly spread through my body. As my thoughts slowly moved towards a mysterious world, I almost forgot about my own existence. It felt as if my face and hands were melting away. My skull was numb and it felt as there were millions of ants crawling on it.

Finally, I realized that I had struck my head on the piece of timber which they placed into the grave during burials. I was in a room covered by soil, a place where the only neighbors were maggots and creepy crawlies. If this was all real; then I was dead and the next life, frequently mentioned on earth was about to commence. Perhaps, the angels of interrogation would soon appear to ask about the terrible life I had left behind. All the things I had done wrong and things I had failed to do would be asked. The heat which was constantly intensifying in my head was signaling a horrific punishment which would even freeze time.

Each time I closed my eyes, scenes from my life that I did not even wish to remember, appeared in my head. Slowly I was developing a strong feeling of regret which was worthless now. It was too late. In my 33 years on earth I did nothing good. Those around me had forgotten to laugh.

I was trembling with fear. I could almost feel the punishment which awaited me. I could sense the ghastly heat of Hell as I watched episodes from the story of my life. The terrible feeling of regret had raised my heart rate so much that I almost forgot about the punishment of Hell. Yes, although I was buried on earth, I was about to embark on a journey of pain and suffering, hauling a bag full of sins on my back. My destination was no other than hellfire.

Something was forcing me to remember my life. I felt ashamed as I went back to my childhood. I was only twelve and my father was drinking with his friends. They seemed really happy and joyful. I assumed that it was the alcohol that gave them this happiness. Each glass they emptied made them more joyful, it was just like scenes I had seen on TV. The shows on TV were confirming my theory as a child. From that day on, I began to share my father's bottle. He was not even upset when he caught me the first time. Instead, he filled my glass and said, "A true man drinks". Later on in life, I got involved in all types of evil with the influence of this Satan that traveled in my blood vessels.

First I started with my relatives and neighbors. Then spread my wickedness to others in the community. In my opinion, people had no value. Moreover, even my father, mother, partner and friends meant nothing too me. I could have easily killed anyone who tried to stand in my way. I was like a robot controlled by a single bottle.

There were a few occasions where I had hit my parents because they refused to give me money so I could buy alcohol. They died in poverty and I was the cause. However, my father had dug this trench of torture with his own hands, when he placed the first glass in my hand. On the other hand, my mother was like a machine that had no other function in life besides housework. Still, I realize now that I should have been good to them regardless. I wish that I had another chance to go back and make up for what I had done to them. I would have begged for their forgiveness.

I remember the day I got married. My wife was not a companion; she was an experimental object which I used for testing my appalling sadistic ideologies. There wasn't a day in which I gave happiness to her. I truly hope that from this day on she'll find happiness. Now, the faces of my children stood before my eyes. These were sad faces that never felt the warmth and compassion of their father's arms. I wonder what terrible things awaited them in life. I wish it was possible for me to go back to them. I would tell my wife and children how sorry I was; plea for their forgiveness and assure them a bright future.

By now I had stopped trembling but my heart rate was still quite high. It was dead calm and the only sound I could hear was my heart beating like a drum. It was as if a mysterious hand had grabbed my internal organs, squeezing them tighter and tighter. I continued to think of all the bad things I had done to people.

Everyone regretted knowing me. At nights I would yell and shout in my neighborhood, knocking on doors and picking fights with people. I even took my children's pocket money and spanked them when they refused. How I wish that I could be given a second chance. I would visit everyone door to door, and beg for their forgiveness.

It was all too late now…I was heading towards an abyss of eternal punishment which I had deserved. A mere 33 years of bad deeds was now sending me to everlasting torment. Very soon, the angels would come to question me about a life which did not even have a single good in it.

As time past, the method of torture applied on my body was changing. Now, I began to feel as if red hot irons were being pressed on my flesh. My bones were being squeezed. My throat had dried up and my lips were stuck to each other.

The most painful part of the questioning was going to be about my faith. They were going to ask me about my Lord and His Messenger. Have you once prayed to Allah, they would ask? I had no answers because I had worshipped the bottle all my life. Every hour of every day I thought of drinking. Even my dreams were made up of alcohol; many times I wished that it would flow from the taps in my house. How was I supposed to answer to the question of, **"who is your lord?"** The only thing I had worshipped on earth was alcohol. I never thought that death would come so early. I wish they gave me one last chance, so I could go back and tell those rebellious sinners who believe that they will never die, what terrible consequences await them.

I did not know whether time had any relevance anymore. I was being subjected to a different form of torture each time I thought about the bad things I had done to different people. This was going to be never ending pain. Even the thought of being dead was so frightening. At that point, I began to scream with fear, one more chance O Lord.. .one more chance!!

Suddenly, I opened my eyes. I was under a bunk in the city park. I must have been so drunk the previous night I had failed to make it home. There was an awful stench coming from my clothes. There were bottles all around me. I decided to pick them up and place them in the rubbish. But I was even afraid to touch them now.

That was the day which changed my life. I purified myself from all filth and submitted to Allah. I became a new man who prayed 5 times a day, loved and cared for his family. Now, when I look at life I only see beauty, which in turn makes me think of good things. For the first time I feel true pleasure and satisfaction.

I continue to think about that horrible pain. What if God had not given me another chance?

CHAPTER SIX

Third word

In the Name of God, the Merciful, the Compassionate. *O you people, worship....*

If you want to understand what great profit and happiness lie in worship, and what great loss and ruin lie in vice and dissipation listen to and take heed of the following story which is in the form of a comparison:

One time, two soldiers received orders to proceed to a distant city. They set off and travelled together until the road forked. At the fork was a man who said to them, "The road on the right causes no loss at all, and nine out of ten of those who take it receive a high profit and experience great ease. While the road on the left provides no advantages, and nine out of ten of its travelers make a loss. But they are the same as regards distance. Only there is one difference: those who take the left-hand road, which has no rules and no one in authority, travel without baggage and arms. They feel an apparent lightness and deceptive ease. Whereas those travelling on the right-hand road, which is under military order, are compelled to carry a kit-bag full of nutritious rations four kilos or so in weight and a superb army rifle of about two kilos which will overpower and rout every enemy... "

After the two soldiers had listened to what this instructive man had to say, the fortunate one took the road to the right. He loaded the weight of ten kilos onto his back, but his heart and spirit were saved from thousands of kilos of fear and feeling obliged to others. As for the other, luckless, soldier, he left the army. He did not want to conform to the order, and he went off to the left. He was released from bearing a load of ten kilos, but his heart was constricted by thousands of kilos of indebtedness, and his spirit crushed by innumerable fears. He proceeded on his way both begging from everyone and trembling before every object and every event until he reached his destination. And there he was punished as a mutineer and a deserter.

As for the soldier who loved the order of the army, had guarded his kit-bag and rifle, and taken the right-hand road, he had gone on his way being obliged to no one, fearing no one, and with an easy heart and conscience until he reached the city he was seeking. There he received a reward worthy of an honorable soldier who had carried out his duty well.

And so, O rebellious soul, know that one of those two travelers represents those who submit to the Divine Law, while the other represents the rebellious and those who follow their own desires. The road is the road of life, which comes from the Spirit World, passes through the grave, and carries on to the Hereafter. As for the kit-bag and rifle, they are worship and fear of God. There is an apparent burden in worship, but there is an ease and lightness in its meaning that defies description. For in the prescribed prayers the worshipper declares, "I bear witness that there is no god but God." That is to say, since he is believing and saying, "There is no Creator and Provider other than Him. Harm and benefit are in His hand. He is both All-Wise; He does nothing in vain, and He is All-Compassionate; His bounty and mercy are abundant", he finds the door of a treasury of mercy in everything. And he knocks on it with his supplication. Moreover, he sees that everything is subjugated to the command of his own Sustainer, so he takes refuge in Him. He places his trust in Him and relies on Him, and is fortified against every disaster; his belief gives him complete confidence.

Indeed, like with every true virtue, the source of courage is belief in God, and worship. And like with every iniquity, the source of cowardice is misguidance.

In fact, for a worshipper with a truly illuminated heart, it is possible that even if the globe of the earth became a bomb and exploded, it would not frighten him. He would watch it with pleasurable wonder as a marvel of the Eternally Besoughted One's Power. But when a famous degenerate philosopher with a so-called enlightened mind but no heart saw a comet in the sky, he trembled on the ground, and exclaimed anxiously: "Isn't that comet going to hit the earth?" (On one occasion, America was quaking with fear at such a comet, and many people left their homes in the middle of the night.)

Yes, although man is in need of numberless things, his capital is as nothing, and although he is subject to endless calamities, his power too is as nothing. Simply, the extent of his capital and power is merely as far as his hand can reach. However, his hopes, desires, pains, and tribulations reach as far as the eye and the imagination can stretch. Anyone who is not totally blind can see and understand then what a great profit, happiness, and bounty for the human spirit, which is thus impotent and weak, and needy and wanting, are worship, affirmation of God's Unity, and reliance on God and submission to Him.

It is obvious that a safe way is preferable to a harmful way, even if the possibility of its safety is only one in ten. But on the way of worship, which our matter here, there is a nine out of ten possibility of it leading to a treasury of eternal happiness, as well as it being safe. While it is established by the testimony – which is at the degree of consensus – of innumerable experts and witnesses that besides being without benefit, and the dissolute even confess to this, the way of vice and dissipation ends in eternal misery. And according to the reports of those who have uncovered the mysteries of creation this is absolutely certain.

In Short: Like that of the Hereafter, happiness in this world too lies in worship and being a soldier for Almighty God. In which case, we should constantly say: "Praise be to God for obedience and success", and we should thank Him that we are Muslims...

1. A prescription for happiness

Wudu and Salah are two miraculous gifts which contain thousands of secrets. Without exaggeration, I believe that one day in the future everyone will perform Wudu. Today, Ghusl is performed by almost everyone in the world anyway.

First, let us take a look at the three biological miracles which occur during Wudu and Ghusl.

a) Electrons are released from the body enabling it to relax by getting rid of tension.
b) It restores the blood circulation system and slows down the ageing process.
c) It helps the Lymphatic system to function at the highest level which is the fundamental essential of our immune system.

Now, let us analyze them one by one.

Static Electricity Balance: Static electricity balance is one of the most essential elements of a healthy body. There are many factors which may cause an imbalance in the body's static electricity, such as contact with plastics, electricity in the air and furniture. Sometimes, as you come out of your car or stand up from a couch, your body feels like an electric conductor, loaded with large quantities of electrons. This condition can lead to many dilemmas, such as anger, discomfort or even psychological problems. The solution is Wudu and Ghusl. No one can argue the fact that the faces of those who frequently take Wudu become more radiant. In situations where water is not available, performing tayammum with soil gives the same effect.

Today, people who are not aware of the facts mentioned above, try to obtain electrostatic balance through acupuncture, by sticking hundreds of pins into their bodies.

Blood circulation system: Our blood flows in a two way stream system: from the heart to the cells and from the cells back to the heart. Within the tissues, circulation occurs through pipes thinner than human hair. In time, these capillary vessels narrow down due to food deposits or other factors; hence they fail to deliver the necessary nutrition to our cells. In actual fact, our arteries are supposed to be flexible like rubber.

How does performing Wudu achieve this?

During Wudu, water applied to our skin at various temperatures causes our veins to open up and close like a wave effect. This in turn, breaks up the blockage (if there is any) sending its fragments into the main stream. As a result, our tissues become refreshed.

These unwanted deposits usually become condensed in our hands, feet and face. Incredibly, these are the main areas targeted by Wudu.

Lymphatic system: Our immune system is based on white blood cells. Lymphocytes (white blood cells) are carried by the capillaries. These little soldiers come into action whenever danger arises. They attack microbes and in particular cancer causing cells, destroying them with their toxic weapons.

Developing cancer or coming down with a viral infection is an indication of a problem in the immune system. Functioning of the lymphatic system is crucial and our capillaries play a great role in this. Performing Wudu and Ghusl supports the healthy function of our capillaries in many amazing ways.

The washing of hands and feet increases the speed of capillaries situated in other parts of the body. The most important territories of the lymphatic system are the face, nose and throat. Washing these parts during Wudu provides a massaging effect and strengthens the lymphatic system.

If you asked a specialist what you could do to strengthen your lymphatic system, whether they are Muslims or not, they will give you a description of Wudu.

The holy Qur'an commands us to perform Wudu: *"O ye who believe! when ye prepare for prayer, wash your faces, and your hands (and arms) to the elbows; Rub your heads (with water); and (wash) your feet to the ankles. If ye are in a state of ceremonial impurity, bathe your whole body..."* (Qur'an, 5/6).

Later in the same verse, the Tayammum is described and the verse continues by explaining why Wudu is obligatory: *"Allah doth not wish to place you in a difficulty, but to make you clean, and to complete his favor to you, that ye may be grateful."*

Modern science has recently begun to understand the meaning of the sentence *'to complete His favor to you'*. Today, we are beginning to realize the amazing benefits of Wudu, and perhaps it is about time that we acknowledge the great gift of health bestowed by Allah.

Salah: Salah is a form of worship described as 'the pillar of religion'. An act of worship is defined by the Qur'an as 'the reason for our creation'.

There are many levels within this prayer of remembering Allah. From an emulation level, prayers can transform into an authentic Salah and then become a type of Mirac. Those who attain this level would not even blink if you skinned them alive, once they say, 'Allahu Akbar' and commence their prayer. On two different occasions, Ali had been wounded during a battle. In order to prevent an infection, his wounds were cauterized with hot iron when he was performing Salah. The interesting thing was that when he completed his prayer, he asked if they had burned the wound yet. Ali had not even felt the pain during his prayer.

Although, in appearance Salah may seem like a ritual consisting of a series of physical movements, in reality it provides many physical and spiritual benefits to human beings.

Physical benefits of Salah: The muscles of the eye cause it to contract and dilate depending on the amount of light received and distance of the object we are looking at. The best way of resting the lens of our eyes is to look at objects from a distance of about 1.5 meters away. During Salah we are recommended to focus on the spot of Sajdah. And this is about 1.5 meters away from our eyes. 40 Raqats of Salah each day means that our eyes are rested for approximately an hour a day. This is a unique prescription for healthy vision.

The joints in our body carry the heaviest burden. Movements during Salah are the best way of rejuvenating their physical condition. It is a proven fact that no form of exercise in the world can be as beneficial as Salah. Also the continuous discipline of worship during Salah protects our joints for life. Electromagnetism plays a great role in the functioning of the heart and the nervous system. Movements performed during Salah also bring these values to an ideal level. In particular, chest pains experienced even by healthy individuals, from time to time, are very rare in those who perform Salah regularly.

Spiritual Benefits: Salah takes us away from the problems of the world at least for an hour a day, providing a breather through the window of prayer.

Just as the Qur'anic verse suggests, Salah protects us from extremism and sins, hence it keeps us away from stress related issues such as greed and gluttony. Everyone who prays will automatically develop a sense of contentment. This way those who pray regularly will be free of anxiety, which is the main cause of mental problems.

The influence of Salah on behavior: In every Raqat of our Salah we recite Surah Fatiha and during the recitation we pledge that only *'You alone do we worship, and You alone do we seek help.'* This statement inhabits our subconscious and slowly we begin to analyze its moral properties. Eventually, this analysis leads to an improvement in moral and ethical values.

Even those who pray in habitual form, break their feelings of arrogance by performing prostration. Arrogance is a most perilous form of human behavior. This unpleasant disorder exists at the root of all conflicts and hatred. Those who perform their prayers in an appropriate manner become subjected to a spiritual grind down of their carnal souls. Therefore, Salah is a form of worship based on good behavior. Salah is an alert guard that auto-controls faith. The faith of people who pray regularly will not be weakened. Through Salah, fundamental illnesses forbidden by Islam, such as hypocrisy and lying will begin to diminish. Therefore, the reality stated by the noble Prophet "A Muslim does not lie" will prevail.

2. Noble Messenger encourages Muslims to pray

Amr the son of Saad bin Ebi Waqqas explains: I heard my father Saad and a group of Companions speak. There were two brothers during the time of the noble Messenger. One was more righteous than the other. The righteous one died first and the other one died sometime after his brother. People told the noble messenger that one of the brothers was more righteous than the other. The noble messenger asked:

– Did he perform his prayers?

– Yes, Oh noble Messenger, they replied.

– I wonder how high his prayers elevated him! Salah is like a clean river that flows in front of your house. Would any filth remain on those who wash themselves five times a day in this river?

Abu Hurayra explains: Two men from the Baliy-Qudaa tribe came to the noble Messenger and embraced Islam. Later, one of them became a martyr and the other died a year after. Talha b. Ubaydullah said, "I saw in my dream that the one that died of natural causes entered paradise prior to the one who was martyred. I was shocked, so the following morning I explained my dream to the noble Messenger. He said:

– Did not the second man fast during Ramadan and pray six thousand Raqats of Farz and Sunnah, after the death of his friend?

In another translation, the noble Messenger adds:

– Between the two there is a difference of distance from earth to heavens.

Ali explains: we were waiting for the prayer time with the noble Messenger in the Masjid when one person stood up and said:

– I have committed a sin! The noble Messenger was not interested. However, the man repeated his confession following the prayer. The noble Messenger then replied:

– Just now, did you not take Wudu and perform your prayer with us?

– Yes... Oh Messenger of Allah, I did, he replied.

– Then this Salah was atonement for your sin.

Abdullah b. Amr explains: A man came to the noble Messenger and asked, "What is the most virtuous deed?" The noble Messenger replied:

– Salah!

– What comes after Salah?

– Salah!

– How about after Salah?

– Salah!

Once the man was convinced, the noble Messenger said:

– After Salah comes Jihad on the path of Allah.

– But I have a mother and father, replied the man.

– Then I command you to be good to them.

This time the man said:

– I swear by Almighty Allah who has sent you as a Messenger to us that I will leave my parents and join the battle.

– The decision is yours, replied the noble Prophet. Amr b. Murrah Explains:

A man came to the noble Messenger and said:

– Oh Messenger of Allah, if I bear witness that there is no God but Allah and that you're his Messenger, and if I pray five times a day, fast and give alms; in which category would I be included?

– Siddiq and Martyrs, replied the noble Messenger.

Enes b. Malik narrates: When the noble Messenger was in his death bed, he repeated the words:

– Be sensitive towards your prayers and for those whom you are responsible.

He repeated these words until his last breath. Ali Narrates:

The noble Messenger asked for a piece of material. He wanted me to write a list of things that would protect the believers from going astray after the Prophet's departure from this world. I was afraid that the noble Messenger might surrender his soul by the time I got back, so I said:

– Tell me Oh noble Messenger, I shall memorize them.

– I advise you not to refrain from Salah and Zakat, and care for those under your responsibility.

In another translation the noble Messenger fell unconscious after giving this advice. When he regained his consciousness he added: "Bear witness that there is no God but Allah and Muhammad is His Messenger. Hell will be Haram to all who testify".

3. A head that does not perform bow before Allah

Satan befriended a man who did not pray. He saw that the man never performed Sajdah before the All-Merciful Allah. Satan said:

– I was expelled from paradise for the one time that I refused to bow down before Adam. Yet, look at you; five times a day, you refuse to bow down before Allah. I wonder what will happen to you.

Those who are reluctant towards their prayers should contemplate on what kind of an invitation they are missing out on and should remember that one day they will appear before Him with their hands and feet all tied up, whether they like it or not.

The notion of "one" cannot be without Salah' should control our lives. We can survive without many things in life; however Salah is the air and water of the everlasting life.

These days, people seem to think it is quite normal to abstain from the daily prayers, they do not realize that they are all jumping into a blazing inferno.

Parents that convey the notion of "you can live without Salah", to their children are committing the biggest act of tyranny. They are pushing their children towards a horrific end. A compassionate mother could not wish for such consequence upon her child.

"A servant's closest approach to Allah is Sajdah", it is a point where the mortal meets the Eternal and attains great honor by speaking to Him.

4. Worship

In His book, Allah commands worship and threatens those who do not listen with punishment in hell. Yet, He does not need our prayers; on the contrary we are the ones in need of prayer. We are all spiritually ill. The eternal power of Allah is the only refuge that will protect us from the burdens of the past and from the fears of the future. The biggest proof of this is the lives of those who do not pray. Their lives consist of stress, depression, psychological problems or sometimes suicidal tendencies. Everything is created for human beings (the earth, the sun, plants, animals, etc.), hence they all serve mankind. Then why were we created? The answer is in the holy Qur'an: *"I have created mankind and the jinn so that they may worship me"* If someone offered us a bar of chocolate, we would obviously thank them. It would be rude not to do so. Allah has taken us out of non-existence. The decision was His. We could have been created as a worm, a rat or a plant. But He created us as human beings and gave us feelings and intelligence, a compassionate family and an opportunity to study. Should we not thank Him? Everything in the universe performs a duty towards their Creator. If a human being refuse to do his/her duty it would be similar to the following example: Imagine a huge symphony orchestra about to perform before a large audience. All the musicians have taken their place as the crowd waits anxiously. As the performance begins, one musician begins to play different tunes making unpleasant sounds. Perhaps this person had consumed alcohol before the performance. Now, could he claim that "I am only harming myself; I am not disturbing anyone else". Wouldn't you think that this man will draw the resentment of all the other musicians, the audience and the conductor? Just as the example, as all existence and mankind worship their Lord in harmony, a rebellious person who refuses to join in, simply because of laziness, will certainly deserve punishment.

Through worship human beings attain the title of 'Allah's vicegerent on earth'. They will live a joyful life and enter the grave as blessed visitors who receive compliments in the Berzah. They will be treated as VIP's in the hereafter. They will fly over Sirat as first class passengers. In paradise, they will be sitting in the protocol. On the other hand, people who do not worship, will be treated no different to a machine that produces nothing but waste. They have nothing to distinguish them from other creatures. On Judgment Day, they will say, *"Woe to us! Those Prophets were telling the truth and this is what God hath promised"* (Qur'an, Yasin).

5. Brake failure

I was not even twenty as I traveled towards a famous hot springs in Haruniye. Those days, not many drivers had the courage to drive through the curved mountainous roads. We got our hands on a small truck and joined up with a few families. We even took our beds with us. After driving for awhile, we entered the mountainous area that had beautiful scenery of green tones. We were climbing a hill leaving a cloud of dust behind us as we listened to the monotonous symphony of the crickets. Thank God that there were no other vehicles on the road because some parts of the road were so narrow that it was even difficult enough for one vehicle to make it through. Driving through sharp curves, we could see stones rolling down the steep hill into the river below. I was in love with this scenery and wished that our journey would never end. The mountain air was so clean and refreshing that everyone kept on taking deep breaths. Suddenly I saw an interesting thing. I was quite shocked by it hence I shouted:

– Look at that pine tree! It has grown on top a bald rock...there is no soil at its roots.

An old man sitting across calmly said:

– What is the big deal...there are so many trees like this in the area.

– What do you mean it is no big deal? Just take a look at the power of Allah, how He has grown a beautiful pine out of a solid rock, I replied.

– Oh...come on now, what has this got to do with the power of God?

– Then how could a pine grow out of a stone. Who created it, I asked.

– No one...why do you need a creator for everything? This is quite a primitive type of thinking, he replied.

– If it was not Allah, then who created the pine?

– Well, perhaps a bird carrying the seed of a pine tree in its beak dropped it on top of the rock. The seed then fell into a crack in the rock. Maybe there was a small amount of soil in there and when it rained the seed flourished, growing roots into the rock, he explained.

– Let us say that this is exactly what happened, isn't there anyone who controls all this?

– Of course not. Believing in a creator in this modern day and age is quite embarrassing.

– How could a man at your age say this? I could provide thousands of examples regarding the existence of God.

Our conversation was beginning to transform into an argument. We had both started to raise our voices. As the old man began to shout, I retaliated with the same tone of voice. Now and then others also joined the argument. It was obvious that this old man was educated; however, he was the only one there who argued against the existence of God. After awhile, the others tried to stop the argument as they did not want it to escalate any further.

At that point we were going down the mountain. For some reason the truck was constantly picking up speed. It seemed as it had gone out of control. On our right there was a steep hill covered with pine trees. On our left there was a sharp hill covered with huge boulders. It was a big drop all the way down to Ceyhan River. The driver stuck his head out of the window and shouted in panic:

– Brakes are gone!

Everyone one was in shock. A few seconds later they were all in panic. Some began to recite the Kalimah Shahadah, others were praying silently. At that point, I came face to face with the old man who did not believe in God. He was screaming, "God help us...God help us!

Incredibly, the truck began to slow down and then came to a complete stop. Everyone felt a sense of relief as they stared at each other in shock.

– What on earth had happened?

– Are the brakes working now?

The driver jumped out of his seat and walked towards the old man and said:

– Shame on you! A few minutes ago you were claiming that there was no God. Then you started to beg for help. Why are you pleading for help from a God you claim that does not exist?

The driver then turned to us and said:

– I am sorry for the inconvenience, there was nothing wrong with the brakes but I overheard the argument and wanted to teach a lesson to this old man.

The old man was blushing as he reflected on what just happened. When we arrived at the hot springs, he approached me and whispered:

– Son, I am truly sorry…I've just realized that I always believed in the God which I had ignorantly denied for many years. You helped me acknowledge this. I am also grateful to our driver for bringing me to my senses.

CHAPTER SEVEN

Fourth word

> *In the Name of God, the Merciful, the Compassionate.*
> *The prescribed prayers are the pillar of religion.*

If you want to understand with the certainty that two plus two equals four just how valuable and important are the prescribed prayers, and with what little expense they are gained, and how crazy and harmful is the person who neglects them, pay attention to the following story which is in the form of a comparison:

One time, a mighty ruler gave each of two of his servants' twenty-four gold pieces and sent them to settle on one of his rich, royal farms two months' distance away. "Use this money for your tickets", he commanded them, "and buy whatever is necessary for your house there with it. There is a station one day's distance from the farm. And there is both road-transport, and a railway, and boats, and airplanes. They can be benefited from according to your capital."

The two servants set off after receiving these instructions. One of them was fortunate so that he spent a small amount of money on the way to the station. Included in his transactions was some business so profitable and pleasing to his master that his capital increased a thousand times. As for the other servant, since he was luckless and a lay about, he spent twenty-three pieces of gold on the way to the station, wasting it on gambling and amusements. A single gold piece remained. His friend said to him: "Spend this last gold piece on a ticket so that you will not have to walk the long journey and starve. Moreover, our master is generous; perhaps he will take pity on you and forgive you your faults, and put you on an airplane as well. Then we shall reach where we are going to live in one day. Otherwise you will be compelled to walk alone and hungry across a desert which takes two months to cross." The most unintelligent person can understand how foolish, harmful, and senseless he would be if out of obstinacy he did not spend that single remaining gold piece on a ticket, which is like the key to a treasury, and instead spent it on vice for passing pleasure. Is that not so?

And so, O you who do not perform the prescribed prayers! And O my own soul, which does not like to pray! The ruler in the comparison is our Sustainer, our Creator. And of the two travelling servants, one represents the devout that perform their prayers with fervor, and the other, the heedless who neglect their prayers. The twenty-four pieces of gold are life in every twenty-four-hour day. And the royal domain is Paradise. As for the station, that is the grave and the journey is man's passage to the grave, and on to the Resurrection, and the Hereafter. Men cover that long journey to different degrees according to their actions and the strength of their fear of God. Some of the truly devout have crossed a thousand-year distance in a day like lightening. And some have traversed a fifty-thousand-year distance in a day with the speed of imagination. The Qur'an of Mighty Stature alludes to this truth with two of its verses.

The ticket in the comparison represents the prescribed prayers. A single hour a day is sufficient for the five prayers together with taking the ablutions. So what a loss a person makes who spends twenty-three hours on this fleeting worldly life, and fails to spend one hour on the long life of the Hereafter; how he wrongs his own self; how unreasonably he behaves. For would not anyone who considers himself to be reasonable understand how contrary to reason and wisdom such a person's conduct is, and how far from reason he has become, if, thinking it reasonable, he gives half of his property to a lottery in which one thousand people are participating and the possibility of winning is one in a thousand, and does not give one twenty-fourth of it to an eternal treasury where the possibility of winning has been verified at ninety-nine out of a hundred?

Moreover, the spirit, the heart, and the mind find great ease in prayer. And it is not trying for the body. Furthermore, with the right intention, all the other acts of someone who performs the prescribed prayers become like worship. He can make over the whole capital of his life to the Hereafter in this way. He can make his transient life permanent in one respect...

1. Salah and Swedish gymnastics

In this section we will explain how a famous method of gymnastics was copied from the first obligatory worship of Islam, Salah.

We must remember that Salah is a Divine commandment hence one should not think of it as a form of meditation exercise such as Yoga or a physical exercise like aerobics. However, with this unique form of worship, Allah also bestowed many physical benefits.

In 1776 a man called Per Henrik Ling invented the Swedish medical-gymnastic. Ling was also involved in divinity when he traveled to Germany as a Protestant Priest. Later, Ling went to Denmark and became a teacher in Copenhagen. He was working at a famous private college that provided education to the wealthy and royal students. In this college there were activities such as horse riding, fencing and athletics, believed to be the sports of kings. During his time there, Ling came down with a rheumatic pain. The pain in his arm was unbearable and it persuaded him to begin a vast research. He knew that the cure would be in some type of exercise, but he did not know which movements would be the most beneficial.

Ling also cherished traveling. Initially, he would make short journeys to local cities but one day he decided to travel to Africa. Eventually, fate had brought him to Morocco. For a European, Morocco was an extremely attractive place. The hospitality, sincerity and friendliness of the local people could not be found in Europe. Especially, the way that the Muslims performed Wudu to wash themselves five times a day was quite surprising to Europeans who had no idea about a proper wash up. As a result, ling found the opportunity to compare Islam to his own beliefs. Since he was a man of divinity, he felt close to Islam.

Ling was a man who was interested in sports so the first thing that attracted him was Wudu and the movements performed during Salah.

He had also studied history of the ancient Greece and collected information regarding physical health. Their suggestions were not satisfactory because it made some muscles work too hard leaving others weak. Whereas, the moves performed by Muslims were working everything from the neck, arms, hands, legs, feet to the muscles in the fingers.

In addition, these movements were repeated five times a day providing great benefit for the anatomy and physiology. Ling began to attend the daily prayers. He was captivated by the moves hence he started to imitate them. He was doing it with the purpose to exercise. He continued for a month. Ling was not a Muslim so he did not know that Salah also provided spiritual health along with physical health. Yet, even the physical aspect of Salah was enough to mesmerize him. The tremendous pain in his arm had almost disappeared in a month. Ling had discovered the exercise which he had been looking for since he was a teacher in Copenhagen. Quickly, he returned to Germany and began an advertising campaign. He was proposing that the best form of exercise for the human anatomy is the one Muslims perform during their prayers. He argued that it is the most efficient systematic workout for the body.

Later, Ling went to his country of origin and established "The Royal Institute of Gymnastics" in Stockholm. His son had graduated from the school of medicine. Joining forces with his Son Dr Hialmar, he invented the principles of the Swedish Medical-Gymnastic.

The fundamentals of Ling's Swedish Medical-Gymnastic which became popular all over the world were based on moves performed during Salah. Without question, anyone who has a conscience would acknowledge the miraculous benefits Islam brings to humanity.

2. Sacrifice

It had been a long day. His eyelids had blanketed his tired eyes as he tried to sleep. It was a difficult task because unwanted thoughts were running wild in his mind. He had never analyzed the events experienced prior to that day. However, the incident he had experienced that particular day was quite different. Just like a video cassette, he kept on rewinding the scene of the incident in his mind to watch it over and over again.

He always regarded himself as a person in high position. This was normal since he was into aviation. He flew everyday and loved parachuting. He was so proud of himself that he barely noticed those around him. Since childhood, he was used to such a life. He couldn't get the attention he wanted from his family, so he looked for it elsewhere. He always wanted people he could control to be around him. He was a thrill seeker who had great ambitions. Sometimes, he would think, "this is why I chose parachuting'.

Aviation was his greatest obsession. He even deferred his studies to become a parachutist. It was a thrill that could not be replaced. Dangerous ventures increased his confidence; he believed that he was afraid of nothing. In reality, he was running away from something. Questions, such as 'who am I', "what is my purpose in life", and "where am I going", were constantly bothering him. So the solution was not to think about them. Consequently parachuting provided this.

He had made many new friends, yet they were all the same, constantly trying to prove themselves. However, there was one amongst them, he was different. He had a calm, clean and honest character. There was one interesting thing about him though; he would spend his spare time in privacy. After awhile, they became good friends. He would frequently contemplate on the realities explained by his new friend. However, this made him aware of the huge gap that stood between them. He knew that their roads would split ahead.

Many days had gone by and they had become professional parachutists. They were like birds flying through the air. One day, his friend said to him, "All this wonderful scenery we observe from a bird's-eye view, has a Creator, you know". Involuntarily, he had replied, "Most certainly". However, in time the realities explained by his friend got him thinking. He argued in his mind, "Perhaps this is what I have been searching for".

The previous night, his friend said, "We are all travelers. Our journey begins in the spiritual world, then we pass through the world of our mother's womb, then we continue through this life, the life in the grave and then we move towards eternity. Yes, we are indeed travelers. One day, we shall return to our maker and be held accountable for the life we lived on earth." That night he kept on repeating these words until he fell asleep.

And the morning had come. They prepared for their daily flight. They checked everything including the spare parachutes. In groups of six, they walked towards the aircrafts. It was quite windy that day. "It is going to be a difficult jump today" he said. "We are used to it" replied his friend. As the aircraft left the ground they both stared out the window. The view was tremendous as it took both of them away into deep thoughts. The aircrafts had finally reached the necessary altitude. Today, for the first time they were going to attempt a new move, it consisted of holding hands whilst they twisted and turned through the air. They were both nervous. Finally, they were over the jumping fields. One by one, they jumped out of the plane. Like birds they flew through the air and managed to grab each other. The planned move had been completed with success. They were both smiling with joy. It was time to break up and open parachute. First his friend released his hands and then he reached for the handle. However, as he pulled the handle, the parachute tangled all around his body. His friend was in serious trouble. In parachuting terms, he had turned into candle. In panic he had tried to open the spare parachute without releasing the clips of the first. The two parachutes had now been tangled together. It all happened in a matter of seconds. There was no time; in shock he opened his own parachute, and then watched his friend hit the ground like a cannon ball. That's all he could remember.

When he regained consciousness, he felt pain in his feet and his head weighed a ton. Like a filmstrip, the entire incident was passing through his mind. Suddenly, he shouted, "Where is he!" They said he died on impact. He began to weep loudly...it couldn't be true, he thought.

As he continued to weep, he imagined his friend's face. He was saying to him, "We are all travelers and one day we will all return to Him".

He felt guilty, so much that he started to shout, "Is that the way I was supposed to learn my lesson, by sacrificing my friend?"

His friend's body was prepared and then sent to his family. But he could not stop repeating the words, "Sacrifice...Sacrifice". Then he walked into his tiny room. He cried and cried, praying to his Lord. It was time to come out as a new man, standing upright. He was not going to let his friend's efforts go to waste. With determination and a bright smile on his face, he walked towards the direction of the sunset.

3. The green suit

I could hear the Azan call as I ran into him.

– It is Friday today, let me take you to the Mosque, I offered.

– You know that I do not go to the Mosque, he replied.

I already knew this because he had turned me down before. Yet, I wanted to know why?

– I know but you never told me the reason, I said.

– I don't know, maybe be I get influenced by people.moreover, I do not want creases in my suit, he replied.

I couldn't help myself as I laughed ironically.

– You are joking, aren't you? I asked.

– I am quite serious...I take great care with my clothes and you probably noticed that I love the color green, he replied.

It was true, he loved green. All the suits he wore were green, only in different tones. He also took great care of his clothes, always made sure that they were appropriately ironed.

– What about when you were a child? Did you not go to the Mosque then?

– Yes, my grandfather had taken me a few times. But I don't think I will ever go again, he replied.

I found his reply quite disturbing as I wished that I had never opened up the subject. He was so sure that he would never go to the Mosque again. We shook hands and separated.

Two months had gone by since our conversation. Someone said that he was at the Mosque. I rushed to the Mosque to make sure. They were right; he was right there, at the front of the prayer lines in the garden. As usual, he was in greens again. Slowly I approached him and leaned over. Then I whispered:

– You told me that you would never come to the Mosque again?

There was no reply. He could not reply anyway, because he was inside a coffin wrapped in green fabric.

4. The salah that takes you to paradise

Uqba Ibn Amr explains:

"We had the duty of shepherding the camels. It was my turn and I took the camels out at the end of the day. One night, on my way back home, I visited the noble Messenger. He was addressing a group of people. I caught the last part of his speech: "Paradise becomes Wajeb to those who take Wudu and perform two Raqats of Salah in total submission, both spiritually and physically." I couldn't help myself, "This is wonderful", I said. Upon hearing this, a man sitting in front of me replied, "What he said just before was even better". I looked to see who it was and realized that it was Umar Ibn Khattab. He continued:

– I know that you walked in recently. Before you came, the noble Messenger said: "When one of you performs Wudu and then testifies, 'I bear witness that there is no God but Allah and that Muhammad is His servant and Messenger', the eight gates of paradise opens for him. He is then free to enter paradise through the door of his choice."

5. Salah wipes out sins

Uthman's servant Harith explains: One day we were sitting with Uthman. It was time to pray and he asked for a bowl of water. After he performed his Wudu, he said:

– I've witnessed the noble messenger perform Wudu exactly the way I have just done. And then he said, "Whoever performs Wudu as I did and then prays Zuhr, all of his sins until Asr will be forgiven. Then he will perform Asr and his sins between Asr and Maghrib will be forgiven. This will continue until Isha and then he will go to sleep. When he wakes up in the morning and performs Fajr, if he had committed sins during the night, they will also be forgiven. These are the prayers that abolish sins.

Those present asked:

– We understand Oh Uthman but can you also tell us about other good deeds?

– Repeating, "Subhanallah, Alhamdulillah, La Ilaha Illallah, Allahu Akbar and Wa La Hawla Wa La Quwwata Illa Billah" are the good deeds.

Abu Uthman explains: Salman and I were sitting under a tree when Salman took a dry branch and began shaking it until its leaves fell off. Later he asked:

– Aren't you going to ask why I did this?

– Why did you do that? I asked.

– The noble Messenger showed me this. One day I was sitting with him. He took a branch and shook it like this and all the leaves fell off. Then he said, "Oh Salman, whoever performs Wudu and prays five times a day, his sins will fall off just like these leaves. Then he continued by reciting the following verse; *"Perform Salah appropriately in two ends of the day and in the section of the night that is closer to morning. Good will abolish evil. This is an advice to those who comprehend"*

6. Salah

Salah is a form of worship that is considered as being at the same level of Kalimah Tawhid. It has a different place by the side of Allah. Those individuals, whose lips move for Allah, find in Salah something that no other form of worship could replace. This is why believers rush when they are called for Salah. Daily prayers performed five times a day are a form of refuge, a getaway from the daily troubles and a chance to have a heart to heart with the Creator. Masjids are places of recess. From these holy places rise prayers, pleas and appeals that draw the mercy of Allah.

If a believer struggles throughout his life to perform an authentic Salah, then all the prayers performed in the past will be treated as genuine. Let us not forget the Hadith, "A believer's intention is more blessed than his deeds". May Allah grant us to perform an authentic prayer at least once in our lives, in which we truly get the chance to feel the spirit of Salah... (Amin)

Only through Salah can we get rid of our weaknesses and faults. Salah guides some of our senses towards the path of righteousness:

Excessive ambition is a destructive feeling. Yet, if channeled appropriately, it can be transformed into dedication on the path of Allah. This means that stubbornness can be transformed into stability or positive persistency.

This feeling of greed is given to us so that we reach as high as we can, perhaps all the way to the gates of paradise. So that we are never satisfied with the amount of prayers we perform. On the other hand, if we break our ties with Allah, we will use our stubbornness to deny God and our greed to obtain more and more wealth on earth. • The verse, "Mankind was created with gluttony", clearly explains this. The only thing that could satisfy us is Salah. Only through Salah we can channel our feelings. Salah enables us to remember our weakness and that we absolutely need the help of Allah. This in turn allows us to refrain from the world and begin to seek the mercy of Allah.

Salah reminds us the principles of faith. Following Sajdah, when we sit for Tahiyyat, we remember the Prophets and send them our Salat and Salam. At the end, we recite the Kalimah Shahadah and verify our pledge. The hearts of those who pray attain tranquility and serenity.

It is quite meaningless and unusual for a person who performs the daily prayers to commit an intentional sin. Salah performed appropriately will prevent people from committing serious sins such as adultery or alcohol consumption. Compulsive sinners will abandon their prayers and those who abandon their prayers will distance themselves from Allah. Sins will diminish the rewards obtained through Salah. Those who pray should flee from sins as if they were running away from a blazing fire. In one Hadith, the noble Prophet states: "There is a curtain between a righteous servant and polytheism and that is abandoning Salah."

Salah also establishes the difference between a believer and hypocrite. Believers feel a sense of joy in their hearts when they prepare for Salah. Hypocrites, on the other hand consider Salah as a burden on their shoulders. During a prayer, the following thoughts go through the minds of hypocrites, "I wish this prayer would end soon, so I could go".

Allah cautions us in many verses regarding Salah. *"Woe to those who dither during Salah, they stand before their Lord, yet they distance themselves"*. Our noble Prophet states, "A time will come when Mosques will be full, but not a single believer will be found in them". Unfortunately, those who do not understand the meaning of Salah stand up indolently and perform their prayers as they yawn.

Salah performed in correct manner reminds us the reality of our servanthood to Allah. Surah Fatiha tells us that we need to be stable on the path of Allah and to ask only for His aid by remaining on Sirat-i Mustaqiym.

Salah is complete form servanthood. It is confession from beginning to end. As one Companion straightened from Ruqu, he said, "Rabbena wa lakal hamd, hamdan tayyiban kathiran mubarakan fih". Upon hearing this, the noble Prophet said, "Angels are in dispute with each other over who gets the honor of recording your deed".

Salah is the first obligatory duty for which we will be held accountable on the Day of Judgment. Those who fail to answer for their prayers may end up in hellfire.

Our beloved Prophet reminds us of this important fact, "On the day of resurrection, the first question will be about Salah. You will find salvation if you performed your Salah completely. There is salvation in other good deeds but if you have neglected your Salah, you may fall into the abyss of punishment."

Allah asks those who enter Hell, "Did you not hear those who called you five times a day to Salah? You lived amongst Muslims; you grew up under the shadow of Mosques, then what are you doing in Hell?" They will reply, "We could not overcome our egos. We could not break our arrogance; we closed our ears to Adhan and we did not care for the poor. This is why we are here, at the bottom of this horrific abyss of Gayya".

Yes, Salah and giving alms to those in need are mentioned together in the Qur'an. Salah plays an important role in self development and Zakat is imperative for the welfare of society. Woe to those who break these two apart! And may Allah give happiness in both worlds to those who perform both.

Salah is so important that even the process of preparation for prayer is considered as part of Salah. The time used up for Wudu is regarded as part of the prayer.

- A believer is within Salah as long as he intends for it.
- Angels argue about recording the good deeds of a believer who performs Wudu in the cold, rushes to the Mosque and waits anxiously for the upcoming prayer. (Hadith)
- Umar narrated the following Hadith, "Deeds are valued according to intentions".
- The noble Messenger was taking small steps when we were walking towards the Masjid. When asked for the reason, he replied, "Each step taken on the path to Salah is regarded as Salah, so I prefer to take more steps. Steps taken towards the Mosque have unique value."
- Allah wipes away the sins committed between two prayers. Allah forgives the sins of people who pray five times a day. Salah contains the index of all forms of worship. It is the sign of humanity's salvation.
- The Prophet valued Salah more than anyone and anything. The amount of Salah he performed during nights had caused blisters on his noble feet. Even on his deathbed, he shouted, "Salah... Salah", and attempted to stand up. He joined his Lord with the words, "Salah.. .Salah!"
- "Nothing is closer to Allah than the moment of Sajdah performed secretly". (Hadith)

- Oh...believer, look for an opportunity to perform Sajdah, because Satan begins to scream in agony as a believer places his head down to Sajdah.

7. Young man, have you ever thought about this?

Everything in the universe is in order. This includes the human body... all the way down to a tiny living tissue. When we think about the anatomy of our nose, ears, eyes and mouth, it would be quite irrational to imagine an improper design.

Then how is it possible that such astonishing harmony formed in all matter from microcosm to macrocosm? It is obvious that we cannot even assume that a meaningful sentence could appear on a piece of paper as a result of an accidental spill from a bottle of ink. How was the great book of the universe, containing occurrences of perfect words and meaningful sentences printed? As suggested by Sir James Jeans, "If you trained an ape – considered to be man's closest relative – to use a type writer, can you ever get it to write one meaningful sentence? Then what an absurd claim it would be to assume that a monkey is capable of writing a passage from Shakespeare? This claim is no more ridiculous than assuming that the magnificent design observed in existence is the product of a blind chance."

Now, let us consider few of the hundreds of conditions that were necessary for the development of the earth so that living beings could exist:

i. The distance between the earth and the sun is approximately 149.5 million km. Can you imagine the consequences for life if this distance was halved or doubled?
ii. What about the density of the atmosphere and its formation from gases vital to our survival.
iii. The percentage of oxygen in the atmosphere is 21%. It would have been a disaster, had it been less or more.
iv. Earth's tilt on its axis is 23.27 degrees. This enables the formation of seasons and protects the earth from freezing or frying.

v. We cannot forget the respiratory interaction between animals and plants.
vi. The delicate balance between seas and the oceans, and also the incredible system of purification indicates to a wonderful order and harmony. As Sir James Jeans states, "Earth's transformation into its current stage depends on the precise functions of systems as many as the number of sand grains on earth."

8. He did not miss his prayer

Zenbilli Ali Effendi addresses the Congregation at the opening ceremony of the Bayezid Veli Mosque:

– Oh Muslims! There are many amongst you who deserve to lead the first prayer in this Mosque. We are not sure who should be the Imam today. I propose a solution. The person, who has not missed a single prayer since his puberty, should lead the prayer. Is there such individual amongst you?

There was silence in the Congregation, so much so that you could hear a pin drop. At that moment, a man stood up and slowly approached Zenbilli. He then whispered into his ear: "I thank Allah that during my years as a prince, a Sultan and during my conquests I have not missed a single prayer."

He was then invited to lead the prayer. He took his position at the Mihrab and commenced the prayer by reciting, "Allahu Akbar!"

This man was no other than the Ottoman Sultan Bayezid the II. This verifies the fact that the quality of a nation is measured by its ruler. The excellence of a cream depends on the quality of the milk. As we gather from the incident above, if we were to filter the entire Ottoman Empire we would discover many similar personalities.

9. Salah in the words of the noble Prophet

- Abu Qatada Ibn Rib narrates: "The noble Messenger states: "Allah the Almighty said: "I have commanded your Ummah to perform Salah five times a day. I pledge paradise to those who continue to perform their prayers. There is no promise for those who do not continue performing their prayers".

- Ubada Ibnu's Samit explains: "The noble Messenger stated: "Allah rewards those who perform a Sajdah for him with one reward and forgives one sin. Their rank by the side of Allah is also increased, so perform Sajdah in abundance."
- According to a transmission by Nesai: "Two Raqats of Nafile (*Tahajjud*) performed before Fajr is more blessed than the entire world"
- The noble Messenger stated: "Whoever, performs two Raqats (four Raqats according to one transmission) of Salah following Maghreb, his prayer is exalted to Illiyun."
- Mugira Ibn Shuba explains: "During the night, the noble Messenger used to pray until his feet developed blisters. They asked him, "Do you have to do so much when Allah has already forgiven your past and future sins?" He replied, "Should I not be a thankful servant?"
- Aisha Explains: "The noble Messenger never abandoned his night prayers. Even when he was ill or exhausted, he would perform them in a sitting position".
- Abu Hurayra Explains: The Messenger of Allah said, "When one of you falls asleep, Satan ties three knots on his neck. With each knot, he taps and says, "May you sleep long". If the man wakes up to remember Allah, one of the knots becomes untied. If he performs Wudu, the second knot is untied. Then when he performs Salah, all the knots become loose, giving him serenity until the morning arrives. Otherwise, he will wake up in the morning as a slothful person carrying a dark soul."
- Uqba Ibn Amr Explains: ""We had the duty of shepherding the camels. It was my turn and I took the camels out to the hills at the end of the day. One night, one my way back home, I visited the noble Messenger. He was addressing a group of people. I caught the last part of his speech: "Paradise becomes Wajeb to those who take Wudu and perform two Raqats of Salah in total

submission, both spiritually and physically." I couldn't help myself, "This is wonderful", I said out loud. Upon hearing this, a man sitting in front of me replied, "What he said just before was even better". I looked to see who it was and realized that it was Umar Ibn Khattab. He continued: "I know that you walked in recently. Before you came, the noble Messenger said: "When one of you performs Wudu and then testifies, 'I bear witness that there is no God but Allah and that Muhammad is His servant and Messenger', the eight gates of paradise opens for him. He is then free to enter paradise through the door of his choice."

- Abdullah as-Sunabihi Explains: "We were on a military expedition to Zatur-Riqa. One of the polytheists had made an oath to his family, "I shall not return until I spill the blood of Muhammad's Ashab." He left his home and began to follow the Messenger of Allah. The noble Messenger decided to camp on the way. The noble Messenger asked, "Who will stand guard?" Two men, one from the Muhajirin and the other from Ansar volunteered. The Messenger of Allah said, "Stay by the passage and be on the lookout." When the two came to the passage, the Muhajirin laid down to rest. The other man from the Ansar decided to pray. At that point the polytheist man caught up. From a distance he could see the shadowy figure of the Ansar performing Salah. Realizing that he was one of the guards, the man took out an arrow and quickly released it towards the Ansar. The arrow found its target, but the Ansar gently pulled it out and continued to pray. Assuming he had missed the target, the polytheist man released another arrow from his bow. The Ansar calmly removed the second arrow and then the third. He did not even take any notice of his wounds hence he continued to pray. Suddenly, his friend woke up. The polytheist quickly fled realizing that there were two soldiers. The Muhajirin noticed the blood on his friend's body and shouted, "Subhanallah...why didn't you wake me up after the first arrow?" His

friend replied, "I was reciting such a beautiful verse from the holy Qur'an that I did not want to break it up".
- Abu Hurayra Narrates: "The Messenger of Allah stated, "Whoever performs Salat-ul Fajr with the Jamaat is under the guarantee of Allah. I hope that Allah does not punish others for this (Those who do not perform Salah with the Jamaat). The noble Messenger continued, "This guarantee will be granted to whoever requests it".
- Once again, Abu Hurayra explains: "The Messenger of Allah said: "Day and night, Angels take turns to be amongst you. They gather during Fajr and Asr. Later, Angels that have followed you during the night, ascend to their Lord (to present their reports regarding your behavior). Allah, who knows you better than anyone, asks, "How did you leave my servants?" The Angels reply, "We found them praying and we left them praying".
- Ammara Ibn Ruayba explains: "The Messenger of Allah stated, "Those who pray before sunrise and prior to sunset will not enter Hellfire". These periods indicate to Fajr and Asr.
- Said Ibn'ul Musayyab explains: "The noble Messenger said, "The difference between us and the hypocrites is Salat-ul Fajr and Salat-ul Asr. They are powerless before these two prayers.
- Uthman explains: "The noble Messenger stated, "Whoever performs Salat-ul Isha with the Jamaat, he has revived half of his night, and whoever performs Salat-ul Fajr with the Jamaat, he has revived his entire night."
- Said Ibn'ul Musayyab explains: "A man from the Ansar was dying. He said, "I will tell you a Hadith and I will do this only with the hope of earning rewards. Once I heard the noble Messenger say, "When one of you performs Wudu and leaves for prayer, Allah writes one reward for each step he takes with his right foot and wipes away a sin for each step he takes with his left foot. So you are forgiven as you walk to the Masjid, pray with the Jamaat and as you walk back. You will still be blessed with mercy, even if you're late to the Masjid. Providing you catch up

with the prayer halfway and then complete the Raqats you have missed. Even those who do not make it in time for the prayer and perform Salah on their own will be blessed with mercy".

- Abu Said-il-Hudri explains: "The Messenger of Allah said: "Allah is pleased with three things; lines formed for Salah, a person who performs Salah in the middle of the night and a man who joins the military for Jihad."

- Umar Ibn Khattab narrates: The Messenger of Allah said, "If a man performs Isha for forty days with the Jamaat and without missing the first Raqat, Allah labels him as, 'Emancipated from fire'."

- Yayha Ibnu Said explains: "When the Day of Judgment comes, the first obligation you will be questioned about is Salah. If your Salah is complete then the other deeds will be taken into consideration. However, if your prayers are refused, then the rest of your deeds become insignificant."

- Ali Ibnu Abi Talib explains: "The last words of the Messenger of Allah were: "Salah...Salah! Fear Allah in relation to those under your service".

- Abu Bakr As-Siddiq explains: "The noble Messenger of Allah said: "Whoever performs Salat-ul Fajr, will be taken under the protection of Allah. Do not neglect this guarantee. If this person is killed by someone, Allah will not stop until his murderer is punished in hellfire".

- Abdullah Ibnu Salman transmits from one of the Companions: "On the day Khaybar was conquered, a man came to the noble Messenger and said, "Today, I made a profit that no one in this valley could ever make." The noble Messenger asked, "Oh...really, what profit have you made then?" I continued to sell and buy without having a break. Hence I made a profit of 300 Dinar." The noble Messenger replied, "Shall I tell you the most blessed profit of them all?" The man asked, "What is that, Oh noble Messenger?" "It is two Raqats of Salah following the Farz prayers".

- According to one version of this Hadith: They asked the noble Prophet when they should command their children to pray. He replied, "When the child is capable of separating his left from his right".
- Enes Explains: "The noble Messenger of Allah said: "Whoever forgets a prayer, should perform it as soon as they remember. There is no other form of atonement for a forgotten prayer".
- Tabir heard the Prophet saying: "Salah is the barrier between a person and polytheism (Shirk)"
- Abdullah Ibnu Shakik explains: "Amongst all obligations, the only thing that the Ashab considered as Kufr was the abandoning of Salah"
- Ibnu Umar explains: "The situation of a person who fails to perform Salat-ul Asr is no different to someone who has lost his family and wealth."
- Bara explains: "The noble Messenger stated: "The mercy of Allah and His Angels is upon those who perform their Salah at the front line. (During a prayer) His mercy reaches as far as the voice of the Muezzin. Dry or wet, everything that hears the voice of the Muezzin will verify this. His reward is double of those he prays with.

CHAPTER EIGHT

1. Youth

On the Day of Judgment, everyone was waiting anxiously to travel to the eternal realm of happiness. There was no concern for the Prophets, martyrs and the great scholars. However, for others, this was a journey that would take fifty thousand years and they were nervously waiting for the vehicle which would be supplied to them depending on the life they lived on earth.

As everyone carefully calculated their own deeds, a group of youth who did not have enough capital approached the Angel who was responsible of them, and asked:

– When we were on earth, we participated in a race. We worked hard and with our efforts and hard work we won luxurious sports cars. We had our hands on fast cars. We want those cars now so that we can travel to our destination.

The Angel investigated the details of the race which the group had entered and said:

– You had your hands on the wrong thing; those cars are useless here.

The group of youth asked:

– What about that group of youth over there? It is said that they also had their hands on something and look at them now; they are flying towards paradise?

– Yes...they did touch something on earth and it was only for an hour a day.

– Just for an hour a day? We spent our days and nights working hard, yet we have achieved nothing. What did they touch? The youth asked.

– They touched a small piece of prayer mat and that was enough to give them a flight into paradise.

2. Obsessive feelings and light at the peak

"I felt as if I had centuries of burden on my shoulders, nothing could make me relax, not even if pleasure rained upon my head", he said.

It was spring time and he was also at the spring of his life. Although there was beauty all around him, he felt no joy and took no pleasure out of life. For a brief moment, he stood up and glanced through the window... Then he turned back and looked around the room. He wasn't interested in people around him, as if it was forbidden to have a conversation with people who had problems.

There was an immense emptiness inside him. Perhaps he was waiting to be rescued. Yes...someone who could take him out of this depressing boredom. It was a strange feeling but he believed that this friend was closer to him than himself.

In the olden days, the only salvation for prisoners in Roman dungeons was to escape to the mountains. At one stage, he felt like a prisoner condemned to the Roman dungeons. Perhaps he too could seek refuge in the mountains. He jumped into his sports car and under the clear blue skies of May, he drove towards the mountains. There was a small town at the outskirts of the mountain. This town had square tiles all over its streets. He drove through one of the streets until he came to a park. Then he stepped out of his car and began to wonder amongst the daisies. It was as if the daisies were smiling at him. Yet, with a stone cold face he walked through them. Briefly, he thought about the flowers. To him, they seemed like children waiting for compassion. Instead, they had received a scolding and were crying silently. This made him sad as a few tears emerged from his eyes. He decided to be more careful. He did not want to step on them anymore. This time his feelings transformed into self-pity as he believed all the flowers were crying on his behalf. Finally, he had reached the peak of the hill. There was no joy left within him. When the Roman prisoners had reached the hills, they would shout, "We are free!" Yet he did not feel like saying this. The Roman prisoners were forced to survive in a dark cold dungeon without sufficient food or clothing. He, on the other hand, grew up in luxury and wealth. Everything he could ever wish for was given to him, yet he was not satisfied. Although he was surrounded with beautiful sceneries, he felt depressed and unhappy.

Yes, those escaped from the clenches of the tyrant Roma were free and happy. What about the souls of those who were enslaved by pitiless uncertainties? How about those who pretended to be happy as they dug graves for their own souls? Imagine the people who were like the living dead.

The human body uses its five senses to understand nature. On the other hand, the soul uses thoughts to sail towards infinity. Those who have restricted their thoughts within the solid boundaries of matter can never find the true freedom they seek. No mountain high enough could liberate these individuals from captivity.

He then began to stare down the hill. The river that flowed through the valley below caught his attention. Nature was so enchanting, but even the cool winds that blew through his hair and made waves through the tall grass did not give him any happiness. Instead, it further aggravated his misery. This was not the way it was supposed to be. How could such instruments of happiness make him so miserable? The answer was quite obvious…as long as death threatened to take everything away from human beings, no one could ever find happiness no matter how long they lived.

He sat on a large rock and pondered, "Even the mountains do not give me serenity" He could not take it anymore. He felt so lonely that he began to weep.

Crying had calmed him down a bit. He was focused on a bunch of flowers that elegantly moved in the wind. At that instant he thought about the artificial flowers which sat in a large vase at front porch of their house. He tried to make a comparison. Suddenly he realized the difference between real flowers and artificial ones was the same as the difference between the life he wanted and the life he lived. "There is something missing in my life" he thought to himself.

There was a red ant passing through, as if it was running towards an important target. Using his finger, he made a barrier on its path. The tiny insect paused for a short while as if it was thinking about a way out. Then it made a move to go around his finger. So he kept on changing the position of his finger to block the ant's path. But the tiny insect continued to make its way around. Finally, he decided to let it go. As he watched the little insect travel towards its objective, he thought, "How do they know what to do?" It was amazing as he then thought about the human brain, "How do we understand and analyze all these things?"

Awhile back he had read an interesting article written by a brain surgeon. It was about the nervous system and the principles of its function. The article argued that modern computers were less complex than the brain of an ant. He couldn't remember the name of the author but he had memorized the article because he wanted to know if it was exaggerated. His father was also a brain surgeon, so he decided to ask him. Suddenly, it occurred to him, the name of the neurologist was Warren S. McCulloch. In the article he stated, "If we constructed a computer as big as the Empire State Building and connected a network of 14 billion units (as many as the units in our nervous system) and used the Niagara Falls as a source of energy, this huge computer would still be a no match for the human brain".

Unfortunately, his father was a brain surgeon who had no other ambitions other than adding a few more zeros to the balance of his bank account. In answering his son's question, he said, "The article is not an exaggeration; on the contrary, it is quite modest. I believe that the human brain could not be matched even if they were to build a computer as large as the earth." Why didn't he mention these facts to him before? He was supposed to ask another question to his father, but he had forgotten to do so on that day. "If human beings are incapable of even producing something as complex as an ant's brain, then how on earth did the human brain randomly evolve into such astonishing complexity?" He knew the answer his father would have given, although he had not asked the question, "Son you must first complete your studies and earn a good living. These kinds of thoughts do not put bread on the table".

He took a deep breath. There was an enormous amount of data going through his mind. Although nature was so complex and multi-faceted, there was an incredible harmony and order. The vaporization of water and then its return to the surface so it could give life to all species on earth... The measured frequency and wave lengths which the human ear and eye were designed to detect... The way that the cool watermelon was sent in summer and oranges that contained vitamin C were provided for us in winter by a mysterious hand... All of these thoughts left him captivated. He believed that this perfect order could not exist in a universe that seemed so chaotic in appearance. Yet, it was an undeniable fact. This was the very source of his apprehension.

Everything in nature was coordinated for life. Yet, living beings played no part in this delicate program. The levels of light, temperature, and the composition of water and the atmosphere were not prepared by mankind. They were already there when human beings arrived. A few minutes ago, he thought about vision and hearing. It all made more sense now. If human beings were given the ability to hear all frequencies of sound and see all wave lengths of light then life would have become unbearable. Just imagine being able to see the microscopic creatures moving on each other's face. Could we have been able to sleep if we heard all the sounds that travel through the air, such as radio waves and mobile phone conversations? Even the thought of such things made him uncomfortable.

He thought to himself, "Everything is perfect...yes so perfect". As he continued to reflect on such issues, suddenly a face appeared in his mind. He forced his imagination and tried to form a dialogue with this face. He felt certain tranquility in his soul as his heart warmed up to this face in his imagination. It was as if someone had lit a light in his world of darkness. He could feel serenity all the way to his bones.

Perhaps, he had found what he had been looking for. He always knew that it was close to him. Yes, there was a unique sense in all of us, and it remained in us until we totally lost our humanity. This unique entity was no other than our conscience. Conscience was a compass that pointed to Noah's Ark in the disastrous floods of philosophy. The hearts of those who took no notice of the screams of their conscience had already decomposed.

We are the people of the space age; we worked hard to attain such technological success. Unfortunately, as we traveled through the emptiness of space, we neglected the emptiness that constantly grew in our souls. We did not learn to listen hence we neglected the screams of our conscience.

However, this young man had not lost these feelings altogether. Although, many years ago, one of his teachers tried hard to rip it out of his heart. "You should not bear such weakness in your heart", he would say. He would even teach him the techniques of terminating this feeling. His conscience was paralyzed but it was still alive.

The thoughts that occupied his mind for a long time had finally reanimated his conscience. He asked the face in his imagination, "Where do these beautiful feelings live? I wish I could go there". Suddenly, a longing voice rose from the deep corners of his heart, "They are not far. They reside in your own heart".

He remembered an episode from his childhood. He was so happy then. The torch of happiness was lit in his heart by his grandmother in his youth. Perhaps this torch of belief and hope was being rekindled in his heart. It was blown out when he was in primary school by his teacher who kept on saying, "Do not observe nature with the eyes of ignorant old people". He was afraid that his conscience would once again fall into darkness. However, this time he was dedicated to repair the damage caused by years of worthless information which was relentlessly fed to him. This self devotion gave him confidence and serenity. "This is it" he said. "I will learn what I need to and I will never fall into the satanic trap laid down by that teacher again. I have found the way to solve the problem. I realize now why a great philosopher such as Nice had lost his mind although he assumed that he knew everything."

Finally, he opened the gates of his heart to its limits, inviting in the spiritual face he beheld in his imagination. It was as if he had abruptly solved all the mysteries of the universe. Gradually, he began to feel lighter and lighter. The chains that had incarcerated his soul were gradually breaking away. He felt the existence of the Almighty Creator who never failed to remember his servants, even though sometimes we fail to acknowledge him.

He stood up on a rock and shouted, "I am free!" He was happy as a small child as he ran down the hill. As he felt the joy and happiness all the way to his bones, those souls who resembled Nero the tyrant, were complaining, "We have lost another prisoner".

3. The incredible efficiency of the human body

Everything in the universe functions on non-bias principles, yet the human body is the center of extreme efficiency. The foundation of this principle is to use minimum space and energy as possible.

Let us analyze this principle by observing it in the human body:

For example, the cell membrane is a thin layer consisting of 100 angstroms.

It is an instrument that acts as a condenser, collecting electrical energy. The thinner the layer the more electrical energy it collects. In accordance with this principle of efficiency, the cell membrane was created as a very thin layer.

A nerve cell has the ability to transfer 2,500 bits of data per second. This means that one neuron cell is capable of receiving 2,500 bits of data per second and at the same instant it evaluates the information without making an error. The amazing system that exists in our brains become more evident when you consider that there are approximately 100 billion neuron cells in the brain.

Our spine is a column of 24 vertebrae. In plain terms, it is made up of 24 pieces. If our spine was made up of one piece, we would have damaged our brains each time we walked.

As stated previously, there are approximately 100 billion neuron cells in the human brain and 3,000 connections between each neuron cell. Imagine if the employees of a large telecommunications company had to deal with so many connections.

It is estimated that a single neuron cell in the human brain is equivalent to 1 million PC's. This means that the shell of our brain has the ability to function as 2.8 million billion PC's. Yet, these estimations are based only on assumptions because the limit of the human brain is still unknown. The human brain is an incredible design of technology that functions in a small space with miraculous efficiency.

The design of our nerves in its cable-like bundles also enables the data to be sent as rapidly as possible. This also makes the electrical signals travel 10 times more economically. Hence the energy used per gram is lowered to 1/10th. In order to comprehend the amount of energy saved, all you have to do is think about the 2 million nerves that go through the spine. It is estimated that our nervous system is more than 450,000 km long. This is approximately the distance between the earth and the moon.

Our liver is not a large organ, yet it performs more than 500 different tasks. Another interesting thing about the liver is that it is an expert in performing all of these tasks. How many people can you think of who are specialists in more than one field?

Did you know that to simulate the duties of the eye we need to establish a factory as big as the parliament house?

In one day, the amount of blood that the heart pumps is enough to fill a large tanker. This pressure is powerful enough to lift a semi-truck to a height of ten meters. The total length of the arteries in the human body is about 200,000 km. How is it possible to fit so many organs in such a small space?

The tear glands in our eyes are placed away from the nose on the opposite corner. In accordance with the principle of using minimum energy there is no mechanical system to produce tears. It is done through a capillary system which does not use energy. Tears protect the eye in many ways by keeping it moist and terminating bacteria.

There is an amazing system which also uses minimum energy. It is the system that allows the flow of tears into the nose. This is done by a special flush mechanism situated in the nose. This mechanism does not use up any energy because it is triggered when we open and shut our eyelids. Tears that flow into the nose also kill the bacteria in the nose. This system also moisturizes the air that travel to our lungs.

If there is a continuous flow of tears into our nose, then shouldn't we always have a runny nose? Well, this is prevented by vaporization. Normally, tears should not vaporize in the nose because the temperature is about 37 degrees. However, vaporization occurs at lower temperatures if there is low pressure. Our nose has the lowest pressure in the body; hence this is why tears flow into the nose.

The flexibility of our bones makes them quite hard to break. This is also observed in trees. The inner diameter of our bones compared to the outer diameter is 8/11. According to physical values this plays a crucial role in its toughness and durability. Using these values, an architect named Cullman constructed the crane.

Our intestines have the ability to absorb nutrition from the food that passes through them. The amount of absorption depends on the size of the inner walls of the intestine. This is why the human intestine is a swirling and churning environment with many layers to achieve maximum absorption. The length of the human intestine is about 7.5 to 8.5 meters. If it wasn't for the unique layers, in order to achieve significant absorption, the intestine had to be more than 40 meters long. As with all organs in the human body, the principle of economical efficiency also exists in the intestines.

Our teeth are connected to certain fibers within our gums. These tooth fibers allow the pressure to be distributed to a larger area during the act of chewing. This protects the roots of the tooth from excessive pressure. Otherwise, the pressure applied on the root would have rapidly damaged our gums. The top arc of the tooth is bigger than the bottom, this is also very important in the process of chewing food.

The resistance of our bones is eight times more than that of wood and they are five times more flexible. The light weight of our bones makes our lives easier. Bones were designed quite efficiently, less material yet more resistance. How did such remarkable design appear? The fingers of a talented artist point to himself.

4. Warnings and admonitions

To the young people who request advice so that they could protect themselves from the dangerous temptations of life, carnal desires and obsessive behavior:

- The **HOSPITAL** spoke in its own unique way and said: "Most of the young people come to me complaining about illnesses and diseases related to bad habits such as smoking, alcohol consumption and drugs. Those who do not understand the meaning of contentment and submission and those who fall into depression due to fear of death also visit us on a regular basis. Of course people in their middle ages and old folks who are almost ready to depart from this world, visit us frequently. I wish I could take you on a tour through my corridors, so you could see for yourself, how people fall victim to minute viruses. Yes...I wish you could see the frosty faces of paralyzed patients and those who lay in coma like a dead person. Perhaps, you could take a look at the relatives of patients who are about to die, crying helplessly beside their beds. Maybe, you can contemplate on the feeble attitudes of close relatives who had just lost their loved one in one of my rooms. Young man, perhaps you had witnessed such scenes before. Besides car accidents, young people who have strong faith, rarely visit me, because their faith protects them from detrimental habits. The old people who have strong faith have no concerns too, because they realize that this world is temporary and that they are about to move onto an everlasting life. Their relatives also display great patience because they know that Allah gives life and takes it away. This faith and belief protects them from depression and acute stress. You probably realized the state of those who have no faith. One day, if you ever need crucial advice, please feel free to visit me and take a good look at the helpless patients and those who lose their lives here. Perhaps this will bring you to your senses. What can I say; I for one believe that faith brings happiness both in this world and in the one after. Do not ever forget that this world is transient and human beings are quite weak and helpless. May Allah help you..."

- The **PRISON** also spoke in its own unique way and said: "You are a fortunate young man because you asked for advice. Most of the young people who come to me have done bad things to others. Once they come here, I realize that they get plenty of time to think about what they had done wrong. And did you know that they all regret their behavior. Especially, the longer they stay, the bigger their regret gets. I hear them say, "I wish I could go back.. .I would never do those things again." You can be sure that even my cold walls feel like shedding tears upon hearing their cries. I always wish that people feared Allah and the Day of Judgment so that they would never come to me... Young man, do not forget that all the beauty you possess comes from Islam. Take a strong hold on the rope of Islam and never loosen your grip..."
- The **VENUES OF SIN** (gambling venues, pubs, nightclubs, etc.) also spoke in their own unique way and said: "Most of the young people who visit us have forgotten Allah. They are not satisfied in life so they darken their souls with intoxication. They are vulnerable people who have fallen into the abyss of gambling trying to win in games that no one has won before. The more they play the further they sink. You should feel sorry for them.

Do not belittle them, because they were not fortunate like you. No one gave them advice. No one told them about the beauties of faith and that disbelief would drag them into a world of darkness and sorrow. You should thank Allah for your situation and pray for those who have fallen into my abyss, so that they could find Allah and save themselves from this swamp." The **CEMETERY** also spoke in its own unique way and said: "Oh curious young man, why do you fear me? You do not need to be afraid, because I am just a waiting room for those who believe. Through me they travel to an eternal life in paradise. I shall look after you until the Day of Judgment and then I will let you continue your journey towards paradise. However, come take a walk with me, I will show you some interesting examples. See that young child there, he is so cute, yet he had to come here so soon... What about that old man. See the way he is resting...as if he needed to unload many years of exhaustion. The reason I showed you this is so you realize that those who come to me can be young or old. I wanted you to be prepared. Now let me take you to the grave of that young man over there. Just be ready now, because it is scary and you will be distressed. He was a person who refused to obey his Lord. You see how his body feels, as if there is a ton of weight on his chest. He is in great stress because he is all alone. Everyone he trusted on this world had abandoned him. I wished that he had done things that would not have abandoned him here. Can you hear his screams of regret? Unfortunately, there is no way back for him; he is on his way to hellfire. I see that your face has gone pale. This is nothing compare to what awaits them in hell. Anyway, I do not want to disappoint you anymore. Let us go to that grave where the beautiful scent is coming from. See the smile on his face. He is so pleased with the mercy of Allah. Take a look at the person with the bright face next to him. He is his friend. They were true friends also on earth. The bright-faced person you see is his prayers. This young man performed all his prayers without showing any lethargy on earth. Hence with the permission of

Allah, his prayers transformed into a friend who would keep him company in the grave. Can you also see those breathtaking things over there? They are all his deeds. He seems so happy doesn't he? The reason for this is, from here he will be taken to paradise and then he will behold the Jamallulah. Taking a human form, the cemetery then placed its hand on the young visitor's shoulder and concluded, "Sooner or later, you will also come here. Take a good look around you, worldly pleasures have no value here. Do not let them fool you. The only thing that will save you here is your good deeds and prayers. Remember, if you need a companion, Allah is enough. If you need a friend, Qur'an is enough and if you need advice, death is enough."

As the young man walked away trembling with the effects of these words, his imaginary friend also disappeared into the mist. He stared at the cemetery from a distance and prayed: "O my Lord, do not release me from your side. Do not let me fall for the false pleasures of this transient world. Turn me into one of your beloved servants." Then he wept and wept...

5. How did Ali perform his prayers?

Ali performed his prayers in such feeling of tranquility that if the world had collapsed around him, he would not have noticed it.

It is said that during a battle, an arrow had pierced through Ali's noble leg and it was stuck in his bone. They could not remove the arrow. They called a doctor. Upon seeing the arrow, the surgeon said:

– I must give you medicine to make you drowsy so that we can pull the arrow out. Otherwise, you will not be able to endure the pain.

Imam Ali replied:

– I do not need a drug to make me unconscious. Let us wait for the prayer, and then you can pull it out as I perform my Salah.

Time of the prayer had arrived. Ali began to perform his prayer. The surgeon cut his wound open and then removed the arrow. He then covered the wound with a piece of cloth. When Imam Ali completed his prayer, he turned to the surgeon and asked:

– Have you removed the arrow yet?

– Yes. I did, O leader of Muslims, replied the surgeon.

– I did not even notice, replied Ali.

6. The man who became Imam to the Angels

Arjefe of Kufe prayed an extra five times a day and performed Salah most of the night. One night a group of visitors came to him after Salat-ul Isha. Arjefe did not accept visitors at night, so he told them to come back in the morning. However, his mother had already invited the visitors in and they continued with their conversation until midnight. When the visitors left, his mother fell asleep and saw an extraordinary dream. She explained her dream, "I saw a large Jamaat. They were all upset with me. They said, "Oh mother of Arjefe... Why did you take our imam away from us? We could not perform our prayers until midnight because we did not have an Imam".

Arjefe had always performed prayers during the night and Angels came to form a Jamaat behind him. That night his mother had taken him away from his prayers, hence the Angels had no imam, so they blamed his mother for keeping him occupied. This is why those of you who perform night prayers may wish to recite your verses out loud. One would hope that Angels may form a Jamaat behind you. It is recorded that many of the Prophet's companions had a Jamaat of Angels behind them when they performed Salah alone in the desert night. We must never forget that we should always perform our prayers so perfectly that they attract the Angels. Even when we pray alone, we should remember this fact.

CHAPTER NINE

Twenty-first word first station

In the Name of God, the Merciful, the Compassionate. For such Prayers are enjoined on believers at stated times.

One time, a man great in age, physique, and rank said to me: "The Prayers are fine, but to perform them every single day five times is a lot. Since they never end, it becomes wearying."

A long time after the man said these words, I listened to my soul and I heard it say exactly the same things. And I looked at it and saw that with the ear of laziness, it was receiving the same lesson from Satan. Then I understood that those words were as though said in the name of all evil – commanding souls, or else they had been prompted. So I too said: "Since my soul commands to evil, one who does not reform his own soul cannot reform others. In which case, I shall begin with my own soul."

I said: O soul! Listen to Five Warnings in response to those words which you uttered in compounded ignorance, on the couch of idleness, in the sleep of heedlessness.

First warning

O my wretched soul! Is your life eternal, I wonder? Have you any incontrovertible document showing that you will live to next year, or even to tomorrow? What causes you boredom is that you fancy you shall live forever. You complain as though you will remain in the world for pleasure eternally. If you had understood that your life is brief, and that it is departing fruitlessly, to spend one hour out of the twenty-four on a fine, agreeable, easy, and merciful act of service which is the means to the true happiness of eternal life, surely does not cause boredom, but excites a real eagerness and agreeable pleasure.

Second warning

O my stomach-worshipping soul! Every day you eat bread, drink water, do they cause you boredom? They do not, because since the need is repeated, it is not boredom, but pleasure, that they give. In which case, the five daily prayers should not cause you boredom, for they attract the sustenance, water of life, and air of your friends in the house of my body, my heart, spirit, and subtle faculties. Indeed, the sustenance and strength of a heart which is afflicted with infinite grief and sorrows and captivated by infinite pleasures and hopes may be obtained by knocking through supplication on the door of One All-Compassionate and Munificent. And the water of life of a spirit connected with most beings, which swiftly depart from this transitory world crying out a separation, may be imbibed by turning towards the spring of mercy and Eternal Beloved through the five daily prayers. And a conscious inner sense and luminous subtle faculty, which by its nature desires eternal life and was created for eternity and is a mirror of the Pre-Eternal and Post-Eternal One and is infinitely delicate and subtle, is surely most needy for air in the sorrowful, crushing, distressing, transient, dark, and suffocating, conditions of this world and can only breathe through the window of the prayers.

Third warning

O my impatient soul! Is it at all sensible to think today of past hardships of worship, difficulties of the prayers, and troubles of calamities and be distressed, and to imagine the future duties of worship, service of the prayers, and sorrows of disaster and display impatience? In being thus impatient you resemble a foolish commander, who, although the enemy's right flank joined his right flank and became fresh forces for him, he sent a significant force to the right flank, and weakened the centre. Then, while there were no enemy soldiers on the left flank, he sent a large force there, and gave them the order to fire. The centre was then devoid of all forces. The enemy understood this and attacked the centre and routed it.

Yes, you resemble this, for the troubles of yesterday have today been transformed into mercy; the pain has gone while the pleasure remains. The difficulty has been turned into blessings, and the hardship into reward. In which case, you should not feel wearied at it, but make a serious effort to continue with a new eagerness and fresh enthusiasm. As for future days, have not yet arrived, and to think of them now and feel bored and wearied is a lunacy like thinking today of future hunger and thirst, and starting to shout and cry out. Since the truth is this, if you are reasonable you will think of only today in regard to worship, and say: "I am spending one hour of it on a agreeable, pleasant, and elevated act of service, the reward for which is high and whose trouble is little." Then your bitter dispiritedness will be transformed into sweet endeavor.

And so, my impatient soul! You are charged with being patient in three respects. One is patience in worship. Another is patience in refraining from sin. And a third is patience in the face of disaster. If you are intelligent, take as your guide the truth apparent in the comparison in this Third Warning. Say in manly fashion: "O Most Patient One!", and shoulder the three sorts of patience. If you do not squander on the wrong way the forces of patience Almighty God has given you, they should be enough for every difficulty and disaster. So hold out with those forces!

Fourth warning

O my foolish soul! is this duty of worship without result, and is its recompense little that it causes you weariness? Whereas if someone was to give you a little money, or to intimidate you, he could make you work till evening, and you would work without slacking. So is it that the prescribed prayers are without result, which in this guest-house of the world are sustenance and wealth for your impotent and weak heart, and in your grave, which will be a certain dwelling-place for you, sustenance and light, and at the Resurrection, when you will anyway be judged, a document and patent, and on the Bridge of Sirat, over which you are bound to pass, a light and a mount? And are their recompense little? Someone promises you a present worth a hundred liras, and makes you work for a hundred days. You trust the man who may go back on his word and work without slacking. So if One for Whom the breaking of a promise is impossible, promises you recompense like Paradise and a gift like eternal happiness, and employs you for a very short time in a very agreeable duty, if you do not perform that service, or you act accusingly towards His promise or slight His gift by performing it unwillingly like someone forced to work, or by being bored, or by working in halfhearted fashion, you will deserve a severe reprimand and awesome punishment. Have you not thought of this? Although you serve without slacking in the heaviest work in this world out of fear of imprisonment, does the fear of an eternal incarceration like Hell not fill you with enthusiasm for a most light and agreeable act of service?

Fifth warning

O my world-worshipping soul! Does your slackness in worship and deficiency in the prescribed prayers arise from the multiplicity of your worldly occupations, or because you cannot find time due to the struggle for livelihood? Were you created only for this world that you spend ail your time on it? You know that in regard to your abilities you are superior to all the animals and that in regard to procuring the necessities of worldly life you cannot reach even a sparrow, so why can you not understand that your basic duty is not to labour like an animal, but to expend effort for a true, perpetual life, like a true human being. In addition, the things you call worldly occupations mostly do not concern you, and which you meddle in officiously, trivial matters which you confuse. You leave aside the essential things and pass your time in acquiring inessential information as though you were going to live for a thousand years. For example, you squander your precious time on worthless things like, what are the rings around Saturn like, and how many chickens are there in America? As though you were becoming an expert in astronomy or statistics...

If you say: "What keeps me from the prayers and worship and causes me to be slack is not unnecessary things like that, but essential matters like earning a livelihood," then my answer is this: if you work for a daily wage of one hundred cents, and someone comes to you and says: "Come and dig here for ten minutes, and you will find a brilliant and an emerald worth a hundred dollars." If you reply: "No, I won't come, because ten cents will be cut from my wage and my subsistence will be less," of course you understand what a foolish pretext it would be. In just the same way, you work in this orchard for your Livelihood. If you abandon the obligatory prayers, all the fruits of your effort will be restricted to only a worldly, unimportant, and unproductive livelihood. But if you spend the rest periods on the prayers, which are the means to the spirit's ease and heart's taking a breather, then you will discover two mines which are an important source, both for a productive worldly livelihood, and your livelihood and provisions for the hereafter.

First Mine: Through a sound intention, you will receive a share of the praises and glorifications offered by all the plants and trees, whether flowering or fruit-bearing, that you grow in the garden.

Second Mine: Whatever is eaten of the garden's produce, whether by animals or man, cattle or flies, buyers or thieves, it will become like almsgiving from you. But on condition you work in the name of the True Provider and within the sphere of His leave, and see yourself as a distribution official giving His property to His creatures.

So see what a great loss is made by one who abandons the prescribed prayers. What significant wealth he loses, and he remains deprived of those two results and mines which afford him great eagerness in his effort and ensure a strong morale in his actions; he becomes bankrupt. Even, as he grows old, he will grow weary of gardening and lose interest in it, saying, "What is it to me? I am anyway leaving this world, why should I endure this much difficulty?" He will cast himself into idleness. But the first man says: "I shall work even harder at both worship and licit endeavours in order to send even more abundant light to my grave, and procure more provisions for my life in the hereafter."

In Short: O my soul! Know that yesterday has left you, and as for tomorrow, you have nothing to prove that it will be yours. In which case, know that your true life is the present day. So throw at least one of its hours into a mosque or prayer-mat, a coffer for the hereafter like a reserve fund, set up for the true future. And know that for you and for everyone each new day is the door to a new world. If you do not perform the prayers, your world that day will depart as dark and wretched, and will testify against you in the World of Similitude. For everyone, each day, has a private world out of this world, and its nature is dependent on each person's heart and actions. Like a splendid palace reflected in a mirror takes on the colour of the mirror, if it is black, it appears as black, and if it is red, as red. Also it takes on the qualities of the mirror; if the mirror is smooth, it shows the palace to be beautiful, and if it is not, it shows it to be ugly. Like it shows the most delicate things to be coarse, you alter the shape of your own world with your heart, mind, actions, and wishes. You may make it testify either for you or against you. If you perform the five daily prayers, and through them you are turned towards that world's Glorious.

Maker, all of a sudden your world, which looks to you, is lit up. Quite simply as though the prayers are an electric lamp and your intention to perform them touches the switch, they disperse that world's darkness and show the changes and movements within the confused wretchedness of worldly chaos to be a wise and purposeful order and a meaningful writing of Divine power. They scatter one light of the light-filled verse,

> *God is the Light of the Heavens and the Earth*

over your heart, and your world on that day is illuminated through the reflection of that light. And it will cause it to testify in your favour through its luminosity.

Beware, do not say: "What are my prayers in comparison with the reality of the prayers?", because like the seed of a date-palm describes the full-grown tree, your prayers describe your tree. The difference is only in the summary and details; like the prayers of a great saint, the prayers of ordinary people like you or me – even if they are not aware of it, have a share of that light. There is a mystery in this truth, even if the consciousness does perceive it… but the unfolding and illumination differs according to the degrees of those performing them. However many stages and degrees there are from the seed of a date-palm to the mature tree, in the degrees of the prayers the stages may be even more numerous. But in each degree the basis of that luminous truth is present.

O God! Grant blessings and peace to he who said: "The five daily prayers are the pillar of religion", and to all his Family and Companions.

1. Reflections on salah

The verse, "Allah is aware of the way you move during Sajdah", gives us some idea about the way our Prophet performed his prayers and guides us on how Salah should be performed. As the Hadith suggests, "We should perform our prayers as he did". However, this responsibility should not be restricted to Salah only. We must always understand the concept of worship and servanthood as it is done during Salah, with total submission and concentration. It is obvious that we could never attain the level of a Prophet and perform Salah on the same degree. It is impossible for us to feel what he feels. However, this should not discourage us from trying. Everyone captures a different level of perfection during their prayers and this depends on the worshipper's sincerity and the connection of his heart to Allah.

Servanthood

I believe servanthood is the hardest thing in the universe. Building an engine, inventing a computer or even sending a shuttle into space is quite simple in comparison to servanthood. This may sound weird to you but my conscience and experience verify that servanthood is extremely hard. Even at times when you feel that you had given all your heart to Allah, you realize that a sense of murkiness continue to take chunks out of your heart. "Oh my Lord, I take refuge only in you, grant us to be your servants and Ummah to your Prophet".

Be like an accountant

Accountants need to count and calculate all account details to the very last cent. Miserly people are the same, everyday they control their money to make sure it is all there. When it comes to worship and deeds, believers need to act in the same manner. Each night we should control our deeds and review our accounts in the worship department. A believer must keep a healthy account because on the Day of Judgment, he will be held accountable for his deeds.

Those who rush through their prayers

I am disappointed in those who rush through their prayers; because I fear the Almighty Allah may ask: "I grant you everything in life and this is how you thank me in return. Is this the way you perform Salah?" I wonder if we could ever find an answer to such question.

Second nature

Devotions should become a habit with us so that eventually they become second nature to us. For example, if you increase a 2 Raqat Nafile prayer to a 4 Raqat Nafile prayer and continue to pray 4 Raqats for awhile, you will become accustomed to it. If one day you happen to miss it, you will say, "Oh my God, I've made a mistake today".

This type of understanding will unearth the hidden abilities which are already embedded in our souls and will also enable us to take control of our carnal desires.

Three important elements of salah

Salah should be our priority in life. Qiyam, Ruqu, Kiraat and Sajdah are all essential parts of Salah. However, the most important essential of Salah is its spiritual contents. Just as the body needs nutrition to survive, the soul also needs nourishment. The nourishment of the soul is Salah. Salah should be a part of our nature. This is the only way that the soul will obtain its nourishment from Salah. For example, you may recite Surah al Kawsar a thousand times and experience a different feeling each time. Then in amazement you will say, "This Surah is so short yet its contents could fill a thousand pages". One should never think of Salah as a burden.

Another important issue during Salah is concentration. When we go to a gym, we concentrate on our exercises in order to achieve maximum benefit. During Salah we also need to concentrate on our spiritual being by purifying our mind from worldly issues. This will enable us to become a person of the soul and heart. Of course we must not forget that the essential moves performed during Salah should be combined with the issues mentioned above.

Another important issue is that we should not change our behavior and attitude by copying the prayers of others. Others may shake their heads or loosen their arms during a prayer. This is not our concern. Everyone is responsible for their own prayers. We should also not be suspicious of the prayers performed by others because they are fulfilling an obligation to Allah. We must never judge others, because putting others under suspicion is a sin. We should always remember that we are not judges.

There is also the important aspect of day to day issues. It is obvious that daily situations and conditions may affect our Salah. However, no matter what the situation is, we should overcome it with our willpower and struggle to turn our hearts towards perfection. We must remember Allah even at times when we are blessed with prosperity and bounties. For example, if something comes between you and Allah, and even if this is a most blessed thing, you should be able say, "I do not want this Oh Lord! All I want is to be a good servant to you".

Finally, the Salah of each individual is different from the next, depending on their level of spirituality. If you described the way you perform your prayers to Imam Rabbani, perhaps he would find it amusing. There is a great difference in the dimension. What is really important here, for us simple individuals, is to open a gateway to understanding the authentic Salah. Do not try to become an ocean when you are only a drop... However, if Allah wishes, perhaps the levels and degrees that we can only imagine may be granted to us only through his mercy.

Salah is the most important form of worship

Muslims should take great care with their prayers. The reason for this is; Salah is the first obligation for which we will be held accountable.

On the Day of Judgment the biggest hurdle will be Salah, not alcohol or adultery. This does not mean that the other issues are insignificant. On the contrary, this statement describes the importance of Salah. Salah, performed in proper manner will protect the worshipper from deadly sins anyway. Some people make the following statement, "Such and such person is a good person but he doesn't pray". This view is wrong according to the principles of Allah.

If a person is neglecting his prayers, he is living at the losing end of life. Compared to Salah, Fasting is an easier form of worship. Hajj is the same. Hajj injects the spirit of worship into one's soul, whilst providing us the thrill and excitement of traveling. Those who did not pray were regarded as hypocrites by the Companions. In most cases, scholars consider the abandoning of prayers as a sign of hypocrisy.

Offering our servanthood to Allah five times a day could increase our level to a great degree. This of course depends on our sincerity and dedication. Do not take Salah lightly, because each day that passes without Salah is like a day gone without religion. Salah is a form of Miraj. However, this is felt by everyone at a different level. Everyone experience their own Miraj. For some, it passes by their feet and for others it comes quite close. The most perfect Miraj, however, is the Miraj of the Messenger of Allah.

Salah and proximity

Salah is a vehicle that brings human beings closer to Allah. As a matter of fact it is proximity itself. Indolence, on the other hand, is a form of illness. If one does not feel discomfort following the period of indolence, this means that this person is in danger.

Worldly thoughts during salah

Question: Often, we think about worldly affairs during Salah. Is our Salah still acceptable?

Answer: The obligation is fulfilled and rewards are still obtained, however, one may not reach the level of Miraj this way. Allah grants extra rewards for those who perform their Salah in an excellent manner and submission.

For this reason, we should be concentrating on spiritual issues throughout our prayers. Unfortunately, our nature does not allow us to abandon our worldly affairs altogether. On the other hand, if we reflect totally on our worldly affairs during Salah, then our prayers will transform into a business office.

Conclusion: We must do our best to keep worldly issues away from our Salah.

Salah is atonement for sins

If performed in proper manner, as the Hadith suggests, Salah will wipe out all sins. During Salah, repentance finds its true form. Although, the regret offered during a prayer is inadvertent, the concept of atonement becomes evident during Salah as one stands before Allah. The crucial issue here is to perform Salah within the necessary principles.

On the other hand, Salah is atonement itself. Atonement exists in all components of Salah, so much so that it is difficult to separate them apart. All types of atonement cannot be considered as Salah but each Salah performed in an appropriate manner is same as atonement.

We do not come across a Hadith which describes a specific Salah which needs to be performed for atonement. This is evidence to the potential power of Salah. However, Salah must be performed in correct manner, so that it provides the required effect.

In relation to the issue an important point must be made here. According to many Hadiths, If Allah wishes, He would forgive all sins during prayers. However, one must feel the discomfort of his sin in the heart and throughout his day so that an invitation for forgiveness is sent. Then he could look for forgiveness in each prayer he performs on that day. This is a great blessing for those who succeed in passing their days in such manner. For this reason there is no specified Salah for atonement. Just as the night of Qadr was concealed in Ramadan, a time of acceptance was concealed in Jumah, forgiveness was also concealed in Salah so that we appreciate prayers altogether. As a result, it is up to us to find it in our prayers and pluck the fruits of atonement.

Sajdah

Sajdah is a place where we display our weakness and modesty by deserting our egos and taking refuge in Allah. The Almighty Allah manifests in such Sajdah.

This concept also exists in Qiyam. However, it is much deeper in Sajdah, because the Hadith states that "Sajdah is the closest point to Allah." This is the secret that lies beyond the prostration of Angels before Adam. We can go to Sajdah at any time, even outside of Salah, as long as we do not turn it into a Bid'at.

Tahajjud prayer

Those who brighten their nights with the torch of Tahajjud will also brighten their lives on the Day of Judgment. Tahajjud is armor, a weapon and a torch to protect us from the darkness of Berzah. It is a secure shelter which shields us from the punishment of Berzah. Each prayer brightens a part of the everlasting life, Tahajjud, on the other hand, is the sustenance of eternal journey and a guiding light of everlasting life. The holy Qur'an indicates to Tahajjud in some verses. *(Isra, 17/79; Sajdah, 32/16 and Insan, 76/26)* – Tahajjud can be performed as 2 Raqats or it can be extended to 8 Raqats.

According to one Hadith transmitted by Bukhari and Muslim, Ibn Umar is grabbed by two men in his dream. The men with daunting appearances then take Ibn Umar next to a deep pit with a blazing fire burning at the bottom. Ibn Umar becomes afraid assuming that they are going to push him down. Suddenly, one of the man says, "Do not be afraid...there is no concern for you". The dream is explained to the noble Messenger by Ibn Umar's elder sister. The noble Messenger states, "Ibn Umar is a wonderful person. I wish he performed Tahajjud as well". The noble Messenger interpreted the dream as... Allah had shown Ibn Umar a glimpse of Hell in his dream, reminding him that something was missing in his life. Hence the noble Prophet indicated to Tahajjud.

A few tears shed on the prayer mat in the middle of the night; prayers performed in total submission; remembrance of Allah whilst everyone slept comfortably in their beds, play a significant role in protecting us from the evil whispers of Satan and destructive claws of sin. The benefits of these acts can only be understood by those who experience it...

A person with bright nights will also have bright days.

Salah, salah and salah...

Salah is not an insignificant thing that we try to fit tightly into our daily schedule. For us, it is the most important work of them all. For this reason, we should approach it with discipline and in a serious manner. Salah should not be postponed or abandoned because of work or other worldly duties. On the contrary, everything else should be sacrificed for Salah.

Salah once again...

Question: Some people use their work as an excuse claiming that they have no time to pray. What would you say about this?

Answer: Faith (Iman) is the foundation of everything, so one should also approach this issue from this perspective. The essentials of Iman shape our perspective and views regarding life. According to this, belief in Allah is the only thing that can satisfy the heart. Faith is an assurance under which the heart will find tranquility. Those who do not believe Allah will never fill this emptiness with anything else. *"For without doubt in the remembrance of Allah do hearts find satisfaction."* (Qur'an, 13/28)

Belief in Prophets is an important issue that saves us from the darkness of the past and from the uncertainties of the future. It is our faith in Prophets, in particular the Sultan of Prophets that enable us to hope for a speedy passage through the disillusions of this world and the world after. We hope that through Prophet Muhammad's, peace and blessings be upon him, intercession, we will attain blessings beyond our imagination.

Belief in Angels gives us a sense of security when we are all alone. We feel constantly under their surveillance and control. With this concept we take control of our behavior and life with true feelings.

Belief in destiny: Believing that everything good or bad, happiness or sorrow comes from Him. It should be a submission in which no other possibility can be considered.

Belief in life after death: It is one of the essentials of faith that enables us to take control of our lives and behavior. Besides the above fact, it has an unimaginable amount of worldly benefits. In addition to this, all of us dream of meeting the noble Prophet in person, and this can only come true in the life after. All the Prophets, Companions and the great Islamic scholars are waiting in the life after. Belief in the Hereafter for Muslims who desperately wish to meet these individuals is a great blessing.

Now, having faith in all essentials of Iman will bring one's level to a certain degree and will provide genuine peace and happiness. From that point on anything that threatens this peace will be challenged with freewill. Also, the continuation of peace and happiness will be assured by regular worship.

So, the answer to the question is that it is a problem which should be searched in the essentials of faith. Because the problem does not originate in worship, it is in faith. Those who possess a mature Iman would not have such problems.

Perhaps, as we search for an answer here, we should also take a brief look at some issues of Salah. Salah is a prayer that reminds us of the essentials that we briefly described above. Salah is a potential reminder and always provides deep spiritual pleasure. It reminds human beings their weakness and poverty before Allah. It shows us ways to solve, even the most difficult problems that we thought were unsolvable. The source of this power is no other than All-Powerful Allah. Let us analyze this by scrutinizing the verses of Fatiha:

Alhamdulillah i Rabbi'l Alamin: Praise be to Allah, the Cherisher and Sustainer of the worlds. From atoms to galaxies everything is controlled and sustained by Him. Why should we lose hope when we have faith in a God who controls everything and protects us from drowning in thousands of events?

Ar-Rahmanir-Rahim: He is merciful and compassionate in both worlds to believers and to non-believers. His mercy overwhelms His wrath. Then why should we lose hope?

Maliki Yawmi'd-din: He is the sole owner of the Judgment Day. Human beings will be questioned about everything they do in life, to the smallest detail. However, the All-Merciful Allah will also reach out to us with His compassionate hand.

Iyyaka na'budu wa iyyaka nastain: Only you do we worship and only Your aid we seek. We stand before your might with our heads bowed in respect. We plead at your door of Mercy. We confess with our appearance that we are your slaves. This is an honorable slavery indeed. You are our Sultan, Oh Allah you are the Sultan of all sultans. We are noble beings hence we do not bow in front of anyone but you Oh Lord. We are prepared to rebel against anything that you are not pleased with. We only want you Oh Lord.

We conclude with the words of Yunus: "What is Janna? A few Huri and some Palaces...give them to whomever that wishes. For I only want you my Lord."

In reality, this servanthood that we perform with pure faith and in total obedience, in order to offer our praises and gratification to Allah for everything He has bestowed upon us, is also a form of confession that states the fact that under no circumstances could we ever repay Him for what we have received, and also that our prayers are insufficient. Salah is a declaration of weakness and poverty by those who have comprehended the meaning of the relation between the creator and servant. Then, how can a person in such state of mind lose hope?

The following verses of Fatiha may also be interpreted along the same lines. Indeed, a believer who has understood the meaning of prayers cannot use worldly issues as an excuse to abandon Salah. This means, along with the truth of Iman, the reality of Salah should also be explained to these people.

Like a sunflower that always turns towards the sun, human beings also complete their cycle of growth by appearing before God five times a day through Salah. The daily prayers enable one's decomposing feelings to flourish again. It is spiritual revival. It is a way of renewing one's oath given to Allah. From this perspective, Salah is the greatest blessing of Allah. Absence of Salah is like absence of the sun. Just as the sunflower dries out in the absence of sunlight, without Salah, so does the human soul. So, in actual fact, we are the ones in need of Salah.

Those who perform their prayers regularly will also take great care in their business, work, study and social lives by refraining from Haram and Mekruh. In particular, the Zuhr and Asr prayers performed in the middle of the day will supply a feeling of self-control and self-analysis. They activate one's self-control mechanism protecting us from doing wrong. Maghreb, Isha, Tahajjud and Fajr prayers are the times of pleading for the aid of Allah.

Salah is an obligatory act of worship that puts one's life into order. For example, a believer starts work following the Morning Prayer. Six or seven hours later he is tired an exhausted. With the Zuhr prayer, he becomes regenerated. Then continues to work until Asr. With the Asr prayer, once again he gets the chance to revive himself. Both physical and psychological pressures disappear. This disciplined schedule also provides more productivity for the workplace. Those who are not aware of these fundamentals of Salah fall into the abyss of discontent and become stressed and depressed.

In conclusion, those who do not find time to pray because of work have closed their eyes to divine realities. Unfortunately, weakness in faith and failing to comprehend the essentials of belief and necessity of Salah drags people into such invalid arguments. The solution and salvation is that we must make the necessary effort to obtain a strong faith and then we must apply it to our daily lives.

2. Rewards of tahajjud

There was a righteous person who never missed his prayers. Each night he would get up from his warm bed to perform Tahajjud. His wife was also a devoted person who never missed her prayers. One day she asked:

– Will women also enter paradise?

– Certainly, my dear wife, women will also enter paradise, he replied.

The lady was so excited by the reply that she fainted. When she regained her consciousness, the husband asked:

– What made you faint?

– I was so overwhelmed that I wished to enter paradise straight away, she said.

That night she saw a great palace in her dream. The palace was so beautiful that she was enchanted by what she had seen. She asked in her dream:

– Whose palace is this?

– This palace belongs to those who wake up in the middle of the night to perform Tahajjud. It is prepared for the beloved servants of Allah, a voice replied to her.

From that day on, this pious women also began to perform Tahajjud every night. She would frequently repeat the words, "It is all in Tahajjud".

Oh travelers of the right path! Mankind was created for worship. Those fortunate people who realize the reason of their existence found contentment in their prayers performed before Allah.

They say that there is a lot in a two Raqat prayer performed in the middle of the night. All the beloved servants of Allah performed Tahajjud on regular basis. The noble Prophet never missed his night prayers hence set an example for his Ummah. Two Raqats performed each night will take you to paradise.

3. Who is a Prophet?

A Prophet is a Messenger of Allah. He is a person who brings revelations from Allah. He is a role model for humanity, an example of what Allah wants in a human being.

Why do we need Prophets?

Prophets are guides. This means, they are leaders of humanity. Not only human beings need guides, even other creatures on earth need guidance. This is a general necessity of all beings. Let us provide a few examples from the animal kingdom first:

Guidance is a natural issue amongst all creatures. Everything is created with reason and a mission. In nature, no creature was deprived of guidance. For example:

– Large fish place guards next to hollow and tight rocks in order to protect their young.

– Wolves mark their hunting territories with their urine. Other wolves that venture into this territory are punished.

– Wild horses form groups of five or six. They never lose each other even if they wonder off to join other groups. When there is a birth and a new member is included into the group, the leader does not permit any horse to wonder away from the group until the young animal begins to stand on its feet.

– Guidance is imperative for birds of migration. These birds have the ability to fly thousands of km without losing their sense of direction. Interestingly, they lose sense of direction when they fly alone. In one experiment, a stork was captured and held back from its flock that flew away towards their usual destination in South Africa. The captured stork was released 5 days after the original flock with a tracking device attached to its feet. This bird failed to find its way. It had traveled so far away from its destination that it was found dead in India.

It is Allah who provides the smallest needs of all beings; would He ever refuse to answer the greatest need of mankind? We can extend the above examples. Allah intervenes in the lives of even the most basic creatures on earth, providing them guidance, sustenance and aid. How could we ever assume that He left mankind, the noblest of all creation, unattended, without guidance and all alone?

Guidance is a natural necessity for all creatures, including human beings. Accordingly, Allah sends Prophets as guides to all of humanity.

Faith is a natural necessity for human beings, hence if Allah had not sent Prophets, we would have asked for them. Allah has formulized and programmed the sending of Prophets, otherwise, mankind would have fallen into various conflicts and debates in search of a way of worship and servanthood. Let us enlighten the issue with an example; various electronic appliances are bought for a certain house. People living there have no idea about the new technology, so they all come up with different proposals on how the equipment should be used. However, there is no one amongst them who has sufficient knowledge about the new technology. If they decided to experiment with everyone's proposal, the electronic equipment will surely be damaged. On the other hand, if someone was smart enough to ask for the user-manual from the manufacturer, all problems would be solved. Hence, the electronic equipment will be used in an efficient way. Human beings are similar to the electronic equipment mentioned in the analogy. There are many proposals on how humanity could find true happiness, yet human beings are not happy. They could easily find this happiness only if they read the user-manual which was sent by Allah through his Prophets.

4. A humanity in the absence of Prophets

If Prophets were not sent, human beings would have behaved according to their desires and instincts. They would have invented their own ways of worship. In order to show gratification for all the blessings and bounties bestowed upon them, some would have prayed day and night and fast for many days. Some would have committed group suicides so that they could go to paradise as soon as possible. Others would have no idea about the life after, so they would have worshipped the world. And some would have gone completely astray and begin to worship transient objects such as money, fame, women, animals, trees and other forms of idols. This is done even today. In order to protect humanity from extremism and deviation, Allah, the Giver of endless bounties, has sent Prophets amongst us. For servanthood is in human nature and we needed guidance in this regard. Hence, Prophets were sent as guides.

Today, it is a known fact that contrary to the Prophets, human beings insist on producing religious conflicts amongst themselves. Imagine that Prophets were not sent at all, the situation on earth would have been ten times worse than it is now.

Just imagine a world without measurement standards. For example, if everyone had their own standard of measurement; if everyone used a different measurement instead of meter, kilometer, time, weight, and so on... This would have been a disaster for the world.

For example, if everyone adjusted their watches according to their own principles, think of a student coming to the class at 10 and claiming that according to his time it is only 7.30 in the morning.

How about a customer in a fabric store who insists on measuring the product with his own device? Whereas, the device he is holding in his hand is about a meter and a half. Would the shopkeeper agree to measure the fabric with the customer's device?

Imagine a driver pulled over by the police when he was doing 160 km an hour. The police ask, "What is your reason for speeding?" The man replies, "I wasn't speeding officer...look at my speedometer, it is showing 90". How could we have order and harmony in such a world?

Unfortunately, the measurements (rules and principles) brought by the Prophets are not represented accordingly in our world today. Most of the rules and regulations are set by tyrants, hence the good is shown as bad and the bad is shown as good. A world that comes together to save a whale trapped between icebergs, turns a blind eye when thousands of innocent human beings are being murdered.

If the decision of what is good and what is evil were left in the hands of human beings then the results would vary depending on power and wealth. There will be no peace on earth. Allah decides on what is right and what is wrong. He then informs us through His Prophets. If this was left to human beings then there would be rights and wrongs as much as the human population. May our souls be sacrificed to He who sent the Prophets.

5. Prophethood

As it is known, Allah has sent Prophets to people from amongst themselves. Some obeyed and followed these Prophets, hence fulfilled their duty in this life and for the life after. They have managed to establish harmonious civilizations and achieved virtuous success. Others rebelled against the Prophets. They preferred atheism to faith, tyranny to justice and inhumane activities over virtue. For this reason they were all destroyed and buried into history.

Prophets are chosen by Allah to guide humanity and to preach them about the commands and prohibitions of Allah. They are all unique individuals who have the mission of showing us the right path. The only condition in becoming a Prophet is to be chosen by Allah. No one has the right to argue about the selection of Allah and no one can become a Prophet by working hard, attaining knowledge and performing worship.

The true mission of the Prophets is to pass over the message received from Allah to their followers without altering it in anyway. In this regard, they fulfill their duties in the most perfect manner. The principles they bring to their followers were first practiced by themselves. Indeed, such a luminous Prophet was necessary for such an amazing designer who had created such a wonderful universe. The noble Prophet is necessary as the necessity of light to the sun. Can the sun be without light? Just as the example, Divinity manifests Himself through the Prophet. Is it possible for the creator not to send a messenger informing his creatures about the secrets of the universe and the purpose of creation, and also answers to questions such as, "where do we come from, why are we here and where are we going?"

Is it also possible for the great Designer, who manifests himself through His magnificent art and blessings to his creation, not to inform his intelligent creatures of His requests and commands through a messenger?

A person's speech is the greatest sign to his existence. Just as the example, Prophets and the holy books are the manifestations of the words of the Almighty, speaking beyond the curtains of this immense universe.

There is no doubt that Prophet Muhammad, peace and blessings be upon him, forms the greatest and the most perfect circle in the chain of Prophethood which began with Adam.

The unique virtues, ethics, morals and qualities of all prophets before him had gathered in him. He was given the title of "Seal of Prophets", making him the leader of all prophets and an inheritor to the origin of their religions. Also, millions of Evliya, Asfiya, Suheyla and Scholars attained their levels through his teachings only. Almighty Allah stated in the holy Qur'an, *"If it wasn't for you, I would not have created the universe"*. It is quite obvious that Allah loves him the most. Therefore, being an Ummah to him is a great honor. Accordingly, we should follow in his footsteps so that as he states, "A reward of hundred martyrs will be given to those who follow my Sunnah in the period of conflicts", can be attained.

In this day and age of conflicts, practicing even the smallest principle of his Sunnah is a sign of strong faith and piety. Even in regular activities of eating and drinking, following his Sunnah will bring significant rewards to those who are in reality acting according to their own nature. This basic act of eating or drinking can be transformed into a Hasene and an act of worship. The followers of Sunnah will then turn their lives into a fruitful tree.

Once again the holy Qur'an states, *"Say (oh Muhammad), if you love Allah, then follow me"*.

The verse is clearly implying that those who love Allah must follow his beloved Messenger. This means that those who refuse to follow him do not possess love for Allah. Obviously, those who claim to love Allah will obey Him and look for the most acceptable and the most perfect way of worshipping Him. Hence, there is no doubt that this is the way shown by the Prophet.

Prophets are the most beloved and the most holy servants of Allah. On the day of the great gathering before Allah, they will receive the most blessings and rewards. And those who have turned their backs on them will regret their behavior upon seeing all the rewards distributed.

7. Did you know?

A Prophet is a person sent by Allah to pass His message and commandments, and guide human beings to the straight path. They were the first people to practice what they preached to their Ummah. They never deserted their mission of Prophethood even when they were harassed and tortured. Zechariah and Yahya were martyred and the noble Prophet was harassed and insulted with acts such as, the filth of an animal's intestines being placed on his head.

Muhammad is the most known Prophet of them all. He had transformed a society that buried their daughters alive, into a society that took great caution to avoid steeping on an ant. He succeeded this amazing transformation in a period of 23 years. This is one of the greatest evidences to his Prophethood. Since Adam, all Prophets performed miracles created by Allah as evidence of their Prophethood. Suleiman traveled the distance of thousands of km in a single day. Moses parted the Red Sea and Jesus resurrected the dead.

The rules and principles they brought, which guarantees peace and happiness in both worlds, is sufficient evidence that verifies the authenticity of their Prophethood.

The level of Prophet Muhammad, peace and blessings be upon him, is proven by the power of his faith, and his position of the highest degree which he holds in Taqwa, servanthood and submission.

Even the magnificent art observed in the universe indicates and testifies to the Prophethood of Muhammad:

1) A new star was born on the night of his birth.
2) In the Palace of Kisra, 14 columns collapsed at once.
3) Most of the idols fell down and were broken in Kabah.
4) In Persia a blazing fire that had been burning for a thousand years was suddenly extinguished (Those days Persians were fire-worshippers)
5) The sacred lake of Sace dried up.
6) On the night of his birth, West and East were suddenly brightened up by a mysterious light in the sky.

7) The valley of Sema was engulfed by tremendous floods.

The Prophets were sent:

a) To serve Allah

b) To preach His religion

c) To be a role model to his Ummah

d) To establish balance between this life and the one after

e) To remove doubts and denials regarding the Day of Judgment

Allah created the universe because of him. The universe is a great book that explains Allah and Muhammad is its interpreter. All Prophets before him had mentioned him in their own ways. Isa mentioned his name as Ahmed. Prophet Muhammad, peace and blessings be upon him, has raised the curtain from the face of death. He has shown us that the grave is nothing but a waiting saloon. He has taken everyone to the fountain of immortality and given them a drink of eternity. The noble Messenger did not know how to write or read. However, his illiteracy is a crown upon our heads. Yes he did not know how to write or read yet the information he brought was verified throughout many centuries and it continues to be authentic as those scientists who come across it say, "Muhammad is the Messenger of Allah". The corpse of the pharaoh preserved in England is an example of this. The Qur'an states, *"Today, We shall protect your body so that you may be an example to those after you. Yet most people are ignorant of our signs"*. Isn't this enough as evidence to the Prophethood of Muhammad, peace and blessings be upon him?

In the holy Qur'an, Allah states, *"For every tribe We have sent a Prophet to warn them (about the dangers of going astray)"* Every Prophet loves his Ummah. The noble Messenger of Allah also holds the highest degree in this regard. In the history of humanity many geniuses have emerged. However, they were all successful in certain fields and branches of science. The Prophet, on the other hand, embraced all units and aspects of life and existence. He carried it all the way up to its limit and guaranteed an eternal place for it. Yes...through him, economy, sociology and establishing balance between this world and the one after had reached their highest level. Prince Bismarck stated, "Without question,

Muhammad is a unique force. It is highly improbable for the possessor of power to create another individual like him". In the holy Qur'an, Almighty Allah informs us that the Prophet is a man just like us, but he was given the mission of Prophethood through divine revelations. (Qur'an, 18/110)

The noble Prophet claimed that he was the messenger of Allah and indicated to a book such as the holy Qur'an. He performed close to a thousand miracles. These miracles are clear evidence of his Prophethood:

1) During a battle, the Companions had only four handfuls of food left. The noble Prophet offered a prayer of abundance and the entire army filled their plates from only the four handfuls of food.
2) He split the moon in half.
3) Water flowed from his noble fingers.
4) The previous Prophets and divine books, such as Torah and the Bible testify to his Prophethood.
5) The most active period for any human being is his youth. It is during youth that most people become active in their thoughts and ideologies. However, Muhammad began his mission at the age of forty. This is another indication that he was acting upon orders.
6) Time is the greatest testifier to his Prophethood. History has clearly proven this and the future will also bear witness to his luminosity. (as we observe the downfall of all ideologies)
6) The Messiah stated, "I will not speak to you no more. Because the leader of the world is coming. I do not possess anything of him." (Bible, Yuhanna, 14/30)
7) Prophet Muhammad, peace and blessings be upon him, represented the following issues at their peak and also became a role model to us:
    - He was a perfect family man.
    - He was an excellent commander.
    - He was the key figure in all knowledge.

- He was a person who solved social problems as easy as pulling a hair out of butter.
- Humanity recognized the essentials of civilization through Muhammad. All efforts after him were nothing but imitations. This is why it would be appropriate to call him, 'The father of true civilization'.

CHAPTER TEN

Nineteenth word

I *could not praise Muhammad with my words; rather, my words were made praiseworthy by Muhammad, peace and blessings be upon him.*
Yes, this Word is beautiful, but what makes it so is the most beautiful of all things, the attributes and qualities of the Prophet.

Also being the Fourteenth Flash, this Word consists of Fourteen Droplets.

First droplet

There are three great and universal things which make known to us our Sustainer. One is the Book of the Universe. Another is the Seal of the Prophets, the supreme sign of the Book of the Universe. Now, we must become acquainted with the Seal of the Prophets, who is the second and Articulate Proof, and must listen to him.

Indeed, look at the collective personality of this proof: the face of the earth has become his mosque, Mecca, his mihrab, and Medina, his pulpit. Our Prophet (Peace and blessings be upon him}, this clear proof, is leader to all the believers, preacher to all mankind, the chief of all the prophets, lord of all the saints, the leader of a circle for the remembrance of God comprising all the prophets and saints. He is a luminous tree whose living roots are all the prophets and fresh fruits are all the saints; whose claims all the prophets relying on their miracles and all the saints relying on their wonderworking confirm and corroborate. For he declares and claims: There is no god but God! And all on left and right, that is, those luminous reciters of God's Names lined up in the past and the future, repeat the same words, and through their consensus in effect declare: "You speak the truth and what you say is right!" What false idea has the power to meddle in a claim which is thus affirmed and corroborated by thousands?

Second droplet

Just as that luminous Proof of Divine Unity is affirmed by the unanimity and consensus of those two wings, so too, do hundreds of indications in the revealed scriptures, like the Torah and Bible, and the thousands of signs that appeared before the beginning of his mission, and the well-known news of the voices from the Unseen and the unanimous testimony of the soothsayers, the indications of the thousands of his miracles, like the Splitting of the Moon, and the justice of Shari'a all confirm and corroborate him. So too, in his person, his laudable morals, which were at, the summit of perfection; and in his duties, his complete confidence and elevated qualities, which were of the highest excellence, and his extraordinary fear of God, worship, seriousness, and fortitude, which demonstrated the strength of his belief, and his total certainty and his complete steadfastness, all show as clearly as the sun how utterly faithful he was to his cause.

Third droplet

If you wish, come! Let us go to Arabian Peninsula, to the Era of Bliss! In our imaginations, we shall see him at his duties and visit him. Look! We see a person distinguished by his fine character and beautiful form. In his hand is a miraculous Book and on his tongue, a truthful address; he is delivering a pre-eternal sermon to all mankind, indeed, to man, jinn, and the angels, and to all beings. He solves and expounds the strange riddle of the mystery of the world's creation; he discovers and solves the abstruse talisman which is the mystery of the universe; and he provides convincing and satisfying answers to the three awesome and difficult questions that are asked of all beings and have always bewildered and occupied minds: "Where do you come from? What are you doing here? Where are you going?"

Fourth droplet

See! He spreads such a Light of truth that, if you look at the universe as being outside the luminous sphere of his truth and guidance, you see it to be like a place of general mourning, and beings strangers to one another and hostile, and inanimate beings to be like ghastly corpses and living creatures like orphans weeping at the blows of death and separation. Now look! Through the Light he spreads, that place of universal mourning has been transformed into a place where God's Names and praises are recited in joy and ecstasy. The foreign, hostile beings have become friends and brothers; while the dumb, lifeless and inanimate creatures have each taken on the form of familiar officials and docile servants. And the weeping, complaining orphans are seen to be either reciting God's Names and praises or offering thanks at being released from their duties.

Fifth droplet

Also, through his Light, the motion and movement of the universe, and its variations, changes and transformations, cease being meaningless, futile, and the playthings of chance and rise to the level of being Dominical missives, pages inscribed with the signs of creation, and mirrors to the Divine Names, and the world itself, a book of the Eternally Besought One's wisdom. And while man's boundless weakness and impotence make him inferior to all other animals and his reason, the means of transmitting grief, sorrow, and sadness, makes him more wretched, when he is illumined with that Light, he raises above all animals and all creatures. Through his illuminated impotence, want, and reason, through entreaty he becomes a petted monarch and through lamenting, a spoiled vicegerent of the earth. That is to say, if it was not for his Light, the universe and man, and all things, would be nothing. Yes, certainly such a person is necessary in such a wondrous universe; otherwise the universe and firmaments should not be in existence.

Sixth droplet

Thus, that Being announces and brings the good news of eternal happiness; he is the discoverer and proclaimer of an infinite mercy, the herald and observer of the beauties of the sovereignty of Dominicality, and the discloser and displayer of the treasures of the Divine Names. If you regard him in that way that is in regard to his being a worshipful servant of God you will see him to be the model of love, the exemplar of mercy, the glory of mankind, and the most luminous fruit of the tree of creation. While if you look in this way, that is, in regard to his Prophethood, you see him to be the proof of God, the lamp of truth, the sun of guidance, and the means to happiness. And look! His Light has lighted up from east to west like dazzling lightening, and half the earth and a fifth of mankind has accepted the gift of his guidance and preserved it like life itself. So how is it that our evil-commanding souls and satans do not accept with all its degrees the basis of all One such as that claimed, that is, There is no god but God?

Seventh droplet

Now, consider how, eradicating in no time at all their evil and savage customs and habits to which they were fanatically attached, he decked out the various wild, unyielding peoples of that broad peninsula with all the finest virtues, and made them teachers of all the world and masters to the civilized nations. See, it was not an outward domination; he conquered and subjugated their minds, spirits, hearts, and souls. He became the beloved of hearts, the teacher of minds, the trainer of souls, and the ruler of spirits.

Eighth droplet

You know that a small habit like cigarette smoking among a small nation can be removed permanently only by a powerful ruler with great effort. But look! This Being removed numerous ingrained habits from intractable, fanatical large nations with slight outward power and little effort in a short period of time, and in their place he so established exalted qualities that they became as firm as if they had mingled with their very blood. He achieved very many extraordinary feats like this. Thus, we present the Arabian Peninsula as a challenge to those who refuse to see the testimony of the blessed age of the Prophet. Let them each take a hundred philosophers, go there, and strive for a hundred years, I wonder if they would be able to carry out in that time one hundredth of what he achieved in a year?

Ninth droplet

Also, you know that an insignificant man of small standing among a small community in a disputed matter of small importance cannot tell a small but shameful lie brazenfaced and without fear without displaying anxiety or disquiet enough to inform the enemies at his side of his deception. Now look at that Being; although he undertook a tremendous task which required an official of great authority and great standing and a situation of great security, can any contradiction at all be found in the words he uttered among a community of great size in the face of great hostility concerning a great cause and matters of great significance, with great ease and freedom, without fear, hesitation, diffidence, or anxiety, with pure sincerity, great seriousness, and in an intense, elevated manner that angered his enemies? Is it at all possible that any trickery should have been involved? God forbid! It is naught but Revelation inspired. The truth does not deceive, and one who perceives the truth is not deceived. His way which is truth is free of deception. How could a fancy appear to one who sees the truth to be the truth, and deceive him?

Tenth droplet

Now, look! What curiosity-arousing, attractive, necessary, and awesome truths he shows and matters he proves.

You know that w ha t impels man most is curiosity. Even, should it be said to you: "If you give half of your life and property, someone will come from the Moon and Jüpiter and teli you all about their world; And will also teli you correctly about your future and what will happen to you," if you have any curiosity at all, you would give them what they wish. Whereas that Being tells of a Monarch Who is such that in His realm, the Moon flies round a moth like a fly, and the moth, the earth, flutters round a lamp, and the lamp, the sun, is merely one lamp among thousands in one guest-house out of thousands of that Monarch. (Qur'an, 53:4.)

Also, he speaks truly of a world so wondrous and a revolution that is such that if the earth was a bomb and exploded it would not be all that strange. Look! Listen to Suras like, „When the sun is folded up', 'When the sky is cleft asunder– '[The Day] of Noise and Clamour', which he recites.

Also, he speaks truly of a future that is such that the future in this world is like a tiny mirage in comparison. And he tells most seriously of a happiness that is such that all worldly happiness is like a fleeting flash of lightening in comparison to an eternal sun.

1. The last pearl in the crown of Prophethood

"The life of our prophet prior to his mission also verifies his Prophethood"

1) The incident that occurred during his birth, the supernormal things observed by his relatives during his childhood and suspicions of wise individuals during his youth was all indications of a difficult mission which he would undertake in the future.

2) Even before his Prophethood, he always stood beside those who were treated unfairly and became a member of an organization called 'Hilfu'l Fudul', to help the innocent people who had been treated unjustly.

3) He did not live a life of luxury or opulence. At a very young age he was orphaned and raised by his grandfather and uncle. He did not have power on his side nor did he have any wealth.

4) Although he lived in an era where sins such as adultery were quite customary, he protected his decency, honor and chastity even prior to his Prophethood. He declares that he had intended to go to two different wedding parties yet on both occasions he fell asleep on the way. It is said that he felt so timid on the night of his wedding to

Khadija that he was drenched in sweat. One must consider that he was at the peak of his youth – age 25 -when he married Khadija, who was a widower aged 40. Those days as people went to battle they would entrust the chastity of their daughters to reliable individuals, and in all such cases, Muhammad, peace and blessings be upon him, was the first person that came to mind.

5) Even prior to his Prophethood, no one ever witnessed a lie, a broken promise or even an exaggeration from him. In this regard, even his enemies testify to his honesty. It is an interesting fact that even his archenemies had given him the title of "Muhammad the trustworthy". During the renovation of Kabah a dispute had erupted between the tribes. They all believed that the honor of placing the 'Hajar ul Aswad' belonged to them. They decided on choosing Muhammad as a referee. He placed his garment on the ground and the sacred stone on top of it. He then proposed that a member from each tribe hold one corner of the garment. The sacred stone was lifted up by all the tribe leaders and the future Prophet pushed it into its spot.

6) Following his days of stressful seclusion in the cave of Hira, he emerged with a great mission. This is another important piece of evidence to his Prophethood. The reason for this is that he was illiterate hence he did not receive education from no one. Coming out of a cave following a long period of isolation and then challenging the knowledge of all wise men, indicates to the authenticity of the divine message he had brought. Yes...the noble Messenger had gone through an inner preparation, a spiritual development prior to his emergence from the cave of light. Then was born like a sun over Mecca to distribute his message.

7) Can you imagine a person who had never lied during his childhood and youth to change what has become second nature to him after the age of forty?

"The enemies of our prophet also testify to his trustworthiness"

1) Those who gave him the title of 'Muhammad the Trustworthy' and entrusted their belongings to him until the age of forty, had refused to accept his Prophethood. By their actions they were contra-

dicting themselves. These people were supposed to be intellectuals who belonged to nobility. Were they then claiming that they had been deceived for forty years? Perhaps, there were other reasons behind their denial. It was not the Prophet who had changed; it was them insisting on closing their eyes to the sun.

2) His enemies were not accusing him of lying, hence they could not refute the message he had brought, so they decided to attach other tags to him. They said that he could be a magician or a talented poet. They could not deny his miracles also, so they decided to associate them to powerful magic.

3) Some of them would say, "Muhammad is telling the truth". But their pride prevented them from accepting his Prophethood. They were arguing, "How could a mission of Prophethood be given to an orphan when there are so many nobles in Mecca?" All they could do is to make excuses to deny his Prophethood.

4) The idol worshippers of Mecca were exceptionally advanced in literature and poetry. It was an interesting thing that they chose a dangerous path by deciding to fight rather than accepting the invitation of the Qur'an which stated, *"You and all of your supporters, come together and produce something similar to the Qur'an, or even a single verse"*. The Qur'an was challenging them in their own field of expertise. All they had to do is to write a book matching the Qur'an. This was clear evidence that the Prophet received divine revelation.

5) The unbelievers chose violence simply because Muhammad had no faults. They could not find the smallest act of dishonesty in the Prophet's life.

6) Another, significant evidence to his Prophethood is that many of his enemies, who had drawn their swords against him, had eventually embraced his faith and became his Ummah. Amongst such personalities were: Safwan, Abu Sufyan, Amr Ibn As, Khaled Ibn Waleed, Ikrimah, Hind and Wahshi. Although they were once archenemies of the Prophet, his spiritual attraction had mesmerized them. Hence, one by one they all came to the truth and eventually became preachers of Islam.

"The prophet's life following his Prophethood also testifies to his authenticity"

1) It is impossible for an individual who has a great mind and magnificent ideologies to keep his thoughts to himself only. Obviously, he will declare his message and gather followers. Let us take ourselves as an example, are we able to keep our ideologies to ourselves? We wish to make them known even to strangers. The most active period of the human lifespan is the time between the ages 15 and 25. The entire world would confirm that violent activities occur amongst young people mostly around the ages mentioned above. Recent history shows that many young people have committed violent acts in the name of their ideologies. On the other hand, the noble Messenger had begun his mission at the age of forty. Without question, he was following specific orders and acting upon them.

2) The greatest sign to a person's honesty, decency and integrity is the unchanging character even after achieving success, victory, high rank, wealth and leadership. Take a good look at his life before and after his Prophethood! His views and attitudes have never changed even after his victories and conquests. Success and accomplishment had never affected him. This is a lucid evidence of his Prophethood.

2. Precious hair

Abdurrahman was a student who attended a boarding school. He was a role model to all students with his behavior, attitude, ethics and studies. One day his long hair was noticed by another student.

His tutors at the boarding school and his parents did not say anything because they assumed that he would have it trimmed sooner or later. However, Abdurrahman let his hair grow longer and longer. Finally, one day the vice-principle of the boarding school called him to his office.

– Abdurrahman, your hair has grown quite a bit, isn't it about time you had a haircut?

As a reply, Abdurrahman shook his head from side to side. The vice-principle assumed that he would get a haircut as he was going home during the holiday break. The vice-principle called Abdurrahman's father and explained the situation to him. That day Abdurrahman came home. Following dinner, his father said to him:

– My dear son…do you want to get a haircut tomorrow? Abdurrahman was an obedient child who would never raise his voice to his parents, but surprisingly he replied loudly:

– No dad, I don't! Then he quickly stood up and ran to his room. His parents were in shock as they looked at each other wondering what was wrong with Abdurrahman. A few days later, Abdurrahman returned to the boarding school without getting a haircut. This time he was summoned by the principle.

– I want you to get a haircut tomorrow! Shouted the principle. Abdurrahman bowed his head and walked slowly towards his bunk. He wept until the morning. In the morning he stood in front of the mirror and said:

– I will not let them separate us! At the end of his class, instead of going back to his dorm, Abdurrahman went home. Upon seeing him, his mother knew that the issue was not solved. She embraced Abdurrahman and softly said:

– You know how much I love you son. Please don't break my heart and get a haircut today.

– Mom, you know that I love you so much. I love my dad and my teachers at the boarding school. I respect you all but please do not ask me to do this, replied Abdurrahman.

– Tell me son…why do you refuse to trim your hair?

– I cannot tell you the reason, but I do not want to do it, answered Abdurrahman.

– Son your teachers are upset with you, please don't do this. Come on we are going to the barber.

Abdurrahman had no other choice. So he went to the barber. As the barber cut his hair, Abdurrahman collected all the hair from the floor and placed them in a bag. Following his visit to the barber, his mother dropped Abdurrahman off at the boarding school. The problem was solved. A few days later, the vice-principle came across one of

Abdurrahman's notebooks. As he turned the pages, he was shocked by what he had seen. A bunch of Abdurrahman's hair was placed inside the book. He wondered why Abdurrahman valued his hair so much. Suddenly he realized the note written next to the lock of hair. He began to read the note:

"I would have never cut my hair if it wasn't for my dear mom, dad and teachers. They do not know that the noble Messenger had stroked my hair in a dream. I would have never touched my hair for the rest of my life.

Forgive me Oh noble Messenger of Allah! I've cut the hair you touched… forgive me!"

3. History and time testifies to his Prophethood

The Messenger of Allah lived like a Prophet even before the mission was given to him. Even his birth was quite unique in many ways. Everyone was surprised by the unusual phenomenon observed in his mother, Amine. She suffered no pain during birth, her son was born circumcised and he uttered the words 'my ummah, my ummah', straight after his birth. Many miracles occurred all around the world at the time he was born.

Throughout his life, he was a decent, honest and chaste man. He would not even attend official parties. Only twice, he had been to a wedding party yet on both occasions he had fallen asleep. He married a 40 year old widower at the age of 25. In an age of ignorance, people trusted him with their belongings and families.

4. The pride of humanity

The poet Necip Fazil described him as, 'It is because of him we exist'. Although, some critics oppose the authenticity of this Hadith, the Qudsi Hadith which states, "I would not have created the universe, if it wasn't for you", strengthens the argument. Indeed, Allah created the universe because of him. The universe is a book which explains Allah, and Muhammad is its translator. Without him this great book of universe would have remained a mystery. We would have lived in it without understanding why and how. We could not have found Allah through the universe hence the universe would have no meaning. Whereas, the Almighty Allah states in the holy Qur'an, *"I have created mankind and the Jinn so that they may worship me"*. According to interpretation of Ibn Abbas, "Allah created existence in order to be known". This means that without the Prophet, we would not have understood the meaning of existence and acknowledged Allah. In this regard, we could say that he was the reason of creation.

All Prophets before him mentioned his arrival in their own ways. For example, Adam referred to him as an intercessor, following his extradition from paradise. He pleaded to Allah, "Forgive me Oh Lord, in Muhammad's honor". Jesus mentioned him on many occasions. Once he stated, "There is a lot I can say to you, for you cannot comprehend. I must go now, so that the leader of the world, the Holy Spirit, the separator of right and wrong can arrive to explain the truth to you."

Just before his arrival and during his birth everything he had said occurred. According to Siyar, all the idols in Kabah had fallen; the columns in the palace of Persia had collapsed, etc.

He was always protected by Allah, even as a child. For example, during his youth, he was helping in the renovations of Kabah. He was carrying stones when his uncle suggested that he should place his garment under the stone to prevent a shoulder injury. As he lifted his garment, his legs became visible. He was so embarrassed that he fell unconscious as soon as someone had indicated it.

At a time when he was harassed and insulted, Allah honored him with Miraj. Even the Archangel Gabriel could only accompany him to a certain level. He had to stop at a certain point and say, "Oh Muhammad! I cannot escort you any further. From this point on, everything belongs to you."

The Prophet was extremely modest. Once, a woman saw him stinting on the ground to have some food. She said, "You are eating on the ground like a slave". The noble Messenger replied, "Can you find a better slave than me? I am the slave of Allah".

Above all, he was a servant. There was a mention of starvation once, when Angel Gabriel was sitting with him. The angel asked him if he preferred to be an emperor or a simple servant. He chose to be a servant.

He was modest on the day he began his mission and modest on the day he entered Mecca on his camel as a victorious leader.

He would solve all problems with ease. This is why Bernard Shaw confessed to his greatness with the following statement, "At an age when we are loaded with problems, I realize how much we are in need of Muhammad who solved problems as easy as drinking a cup of coffee".

In conclusion, our Prophet was born pure, lived a pure life and when he had completed his mission, he died with a pure soul.

5. Body in the hands of spirituality

Here is a striking memory from a Muslim doctor:

As a cancer specialist who had forty years of experience in the field, I have witnessed many beyond matter incidents. I have an archive of these metaphysical occurrences. I would like to mention one particular incident that occurred in 1976:

I was a head doctor in the Cancer Hospital. There was a young patient by the name of Serap. She had breast cancer. She had planned to go to Europe for treatment but because of certain formalities, she never got the opportunity. I took special care with Serap and began to treat her personally. After awhile, with the permission of Allah, she began to show signs of recovery. However, as with all cancer patients, she also needed to take great care of herself, at least for the next five years. Serap was a business woman, and four years on, from the commencement of her treatment, she needed to travel to Izmir. She was supposed to bid for an important contract. It was during winter so I gave her permission with the condition that she would travel by plane. Unfortunately, she couldn't find tickets and without notifying me, she had taken the bus. On the way, the bus was involved in a small accident and they had to wait in freezing conditions for six hours. Upon her return, we discovered that the illness had spread to her lungs and bones. The bones in her legs were the worse affected areas. After awhile, she could not walk anymore. Also, we had to attach her to an oxygen device due to the condition of her lungs. She was breathing oxygen after each sentence she spoke. There was nothing we could do for her anymore and she was discharged to her home. The treatment would continue at home. One day, as I visited Serap, she said:

– Doctor, you broke my heart.

– Why? I asked in confusion.

– I've heard that you were a religious person. Why didn't you tell me about God... and life after death? She replied.

I knew that her faith was quite weak, so I was quite surprised by the question. I tried not to upset her and replied softly:

– It is easy to find a good doctor; all you have to do is pay. However, treatment of the soul is different; it must be desired from the heart.

She didn't have the energy to talk anymore, so she nodded her head to say that she desired knowledge. From that day on, along with a fruitless medical treatment, I had started a treatment of faith which was the only prescription for eternal life and happiness. Serap was living her last days, so our tutorials became quite compact. She was listening with incredible attention and from time to time she would ask questions. A week prior to her death, she asked:

– What should I say... at the last moment?

– You have made wonderful progress. Kalimah Shahadah may be too long for you. So I suggest that you say, Muhammad, in your last breath. I replied.

She smiled and nodded her head as a sign of acknowledgment. Serap was in great pain so we continuously gave her morphine which put her to sleep. That week I had to travel away from the city on a business trip, so I couldn't visit her. Her mother called upon my return:

– Serap refuses to take her morphine. She suffers all night.

Quickly, I rush to her house and asked why she was refusing to take morphine. Her answer would haunt me for the rest of my life.

What if I die under the affect of morphine? I would be sedated and I cannot say, Muhammad!

Serap was a special lady. She requested Istihara from me and if there was a sign that she would live for a few more days, she would take morphine in small dozes. I was not accustomed to doing this but one Friday night I decided to perform her request. Allah must have accepted her sincerity and in my dream I saw that she would live till Tuesday. Next day, I said to her:

– Take your morphine and do not be afraid.

This meeting seemed like a farewell. Hence she asked me one last question:

– Doctor... how will Azrail (angel of death) appear to me?

– My dear girl, he is an angel. So he will appear as a handsome prince to you. I replied.

On Tuesday, I was informed that Serap's condition had worsened. I rushed to her house. Unfortunately, I was too late. Her family was in great distress. There was an old female relative who had been looking after her. She was a religious person who approached me and said:

– Doctor, I have witnessed a miracle just before you arrived. An hour ago, Serap took her oxygen mask off and stood up. We were told that it was impossible for her to walk again, yet she went to the bathroom and performed Ghusl. She then prayed two Raqats of Salah. The entire family was in shock. Then she sat on her bed and recited the Kalimah Shahadah. Doctor...just before her death, she said: "Tell the doctor when he arrives that Azrail is much more handsome than he had described".

That was the day Serap had embarked on her journey towards eternity. I sat down with the entire family and recorded everything that occurred.

As I remember Serap with the mercy of Allah, I ask you:

Would the noble messenger who cried saying "my community" at the time of his birth, abandon someone who endured such agony by refusing to take painkillers so that she could recite his name? Most certainly, he was by her side until the end.

6. Lost letter

Ever since she was a child, she wanted to be a Hafiz. She had finally achieved it. Even before completing her university degree, she dreamed of visiting the house of God and the town of the noble messenger. She dreamt of this, day and night, and prayed that it would come true. She knew that she could only go there if there was an invitation by her creator. She always completed her prayers with the words, "Please invite me there Oh Lord".

One day, a friend suggested, "If you can't go there, then why don't you write a letter to the noble messenger?" Upon such suggestion, she thought to herself, "Who am I to write a letter to him?"

She could never have the courage to do such a thing, because she had never felt close enough to the noble messenger.

Yet, the great individual was so compassionate that he knew about all those who loved him. As all lovers did, she also loved the person who was loved by everyone, so much so that she knew she would get a response. She knew this because, she loved everyone who loved her and responded to their affection. The best way of showing your love towards the noble Prophet was to behave as he did and follow in his footsteps. And this required great care and devotion.

Yes…the love of everyone would have sensed her love and perhaps read her thoughts. Sending a piece of herself to the noble messenger made her quite emotional.

She was excited as she sat on her bed with a piece of paper and a pen. She was ready to write her feelings to the person who was the reason for her existence. At that point, she entered into a new dimension. Her feelings flowed through the ink onto the paper which she had carefully selected. The letter was marked with her tear drops as she placed it in an envelope. Her hands shook with excitement as she prepared her message to the person she loved and respected throughout her life.

She had completed everything and a sense of relief came over her. She was in mixed emotions. Feeling excited for writing a letter to the noble messenger and sad for being unable to visit him at the same time.

She had written her letter on rose colored paper because rose was the symbol of the noble messenger. She had also added some dried rose leaves as a gift from Anatolia. Everything was ready. She squeezed the envelope on her chest and then placed it in her bag. It was time to send the letter. She looked for friends who were going to Hajj this year. She remembered her friend Huriye's mother, and rushed to their house. Unfortunately, she did not make it in time. They had already left as she sat on their doorsteps in agony. She felt great disappointment as tears ran down her face.

After sitting in that position for quite awhile she decided to go home. As she got on the bus, she came across her friend Zeynep. Zeynep told her not to worry because her grandmother was also planning to go there soon. This was great news as she decided to give the letter to her. Unfortunately, as they came to the bus stop she had forgotten to give Zeynep the letter.

Maybe I do not deserve to be granted with such an honor, she thought to herself. As she got off the bus she went directly to her other friend, Hurinisa. Her friend greeted her with excitement. She soon realized that her husband was also about the leave for the holy land.

She felt a bit embarrassed but could not help herself and asked if he would be able to take her letter along. A few minutes later she found out that Abdurrahman was happy to take her letter with him. She felt so much joy that tears poured out of her eyes. Finally, her wish had come true.

Abdurrahman took the letter and placed it in his suitcase, thinking that, "Trust is the sign of a believer. This is a letter from one lover to another so I need to take great care of it".

Abdurrahman finally arrived at the town where civilization had originated. He waited for a suitable time so that he could visit the tomb of the noble Prophet and leave the letter by his side. Unfortunately, it was quite difficult to find the chance to pass through the enormous crowd. Each of his attempts had failed. It was his last day in Medina and he was feeling great disappointment for failing to deliver the letter. Finally, he decided to leave the letter in one corner of this holy town. He opened his suitcase gently and reached for the letter that emitted a rosy scent each time he had opened his case. To his surprise the letter was gone. Could it be that someone had broken into his suitcase? But, this did not make any sense to him because, why would the thief steal a letter? After the shock he remembered his wallet and passport. Quickly he emptied the suitcase, only to find that everything was there. No one could have taken the letter. Nervously, he stared at his suitcase. He was saddened by the whole affair as people waited for him. Slowly, he packed his bags and left the building.

The plane had landed in Istanbul but he could not take his mind off the letter. He explained everything to his spouse and said, "The owner of the letter must have picked it up before I had a chance to deliver it". He sincerely believed that a letter written with such affection and emotion could not have been lost. The letter he had failed to deliver was more valuable than worldly wealth and the power that took the letter from the suitcase must have delivered it to its owner.

She had declared her love for the Prophet in her precious letter: "Oh the pearl of humanity.

I love you so much. Next to those who gave their lives for you, and those who walked beside you in the desert, these are only words. However, believe me that I wish to do something and I plead for a Dua from you. Please make Dua to Allah so that He accepts my Dua. If Allah gives me the wisdom and knowledge, I give my word that I shall try to teach it to everyone as long as I live.

Oh the person who I love so much even though I have never seen you! Please ask for the following things from Allah on my behalf. I wish to be a servant of Allah in His religion. I wish to attain the attribute of knowledge which He loves the most. I pray for an intelligent mind, strong will and blessed knowledge. I wish to be included amongst the beloved servants of Allah. I pray that Allah wipes out all evil feelings from my heart and replaces them with His and your love, Oh noble messenger! I pray that He accepts my prayers.

CHAPTER ELEVEN

1. Miracles of the Messenger of Allah

The splitting of the moon

Abdullah Ibn Masud explains:
One night we were at Mina when the moon split in half. One half of the moon was on one side of the mountain and the other was on the other side. The noble Messenger then said: "Bear witness!"

The blessing of food

Enes Ibn Malik explains:

Abu Talha asked Ummu Sulaym, "I could not clearly hear what the noble Prophet said. I think he is hungry. Do you have any rations with you?

Ummu Sulaym replied, "Yes, I do", and then took a piece of barley bread out of her bag. She then wrapped the bread in one of her scarves and placed it under my garment. I took the bread to the noble Messenger. He was at the mosque sitting with the Jamaat. I stood next to them. The noble Messenger said:

– Did Abu Talha send you?

– Yes, I replied.

– Did you bring food, he asked.

– Yes, I said once again.

The noble Messenger then asked everyone to stand up. I escorted them back to Talha's house. Abu Talha saw us coming and said to Ummu Sulaym:

– Ummu Sulaym, the noble Messenger arrived with the Jamaat. But we do not have enough food to offer. Ummu Sulaym replied:

– Allah and His Messenger know best. Then Talha came next to the Prophet. The noble Messenger entered the house with Talha. The Prophet of Allah then said:

– Oh Ummu Suleym, bring what you have. The noble Messenger asked them to break the bread into smaller pieces. Ummu Suleym served some oil with the bread. Then with the permission of Allah, the noble Messenger spoke a few words about the bread. The noble Messenger then asked Talha for permission so that ten people could enter. Talha gave them permission. They all ate and filled their tummies and left. Once again, the noble Prophet said, "Give permission to another ten". They too ate and satisfied their hunger. That day, about eighty people ate and satisfied their hunger at the house of Talha.

In a Hadith recorded in Bukhari and Muslim, Abdurrahman b. Abu Bakr explains:

– I was on a military expedition with the noble Messenger. There were one hundred and thirty of us. The noble Messenger asked:

– Have any of you brought food? A man had a handful of flour in his bag. Quickly, we prepared the dough. Then a nonbeliever came next to us with his herd of sheep. The noble Messenger asked:

– Are they for sale or did you bring a gift?

– They are for sale, replied the man. The noble Messenger then purchased a sheep from the man and we slaughtered it. He asked us to fry the liver. I swear by Almighty Allah, he gave each man a piece from the liver and reserved some for those who were not there yet. Then he divided the meat into two separate bowls. 130 of us ate the meat and the bowls remained full (as if no one had touched them). According to another Hadith in Bukhari, Jabir Ibn Abdullah narrated a similar incident during the battle of Handaq. On this particular occasion, the food was eaten by a thousand Companions.

The water miracles

The noble Prophet was at Zarwa with his Ashab when he asked for a bowl of water. Then he placed his hand in the water. Suddenly, water began to flow through his fingers. Then one by one the Companions took Wudu from it. The narrator asked:

– How many people performed Wudu, Oh Abu Hamza? (this is the title of Enes)

– There were about three hundred of them, replied Enes.

At Hudaybiya people complained about the shortage of water to the noble Prophet. The noble Messenger then pulled an arrow out of his sack. He asked them to place it in the well of Samad. At that instant, the well began to overflow. The water continued to flow out of the well until the Companions had satisfied their thirst.

Curing the sick and the wounded

According to a transmission from Bukhari and Muslim, the noble Messenger asked for the whereabouts of Ali at Khaybar. The Ashab replied:

– He has a Problem with his eyes, Oh noble Messenger.

– Send him to me at once, said the Messenger of Allah.

Ashab brought Ali next to the Prophet. The noble Messenger applied his saliva on Ali's eyes and made Dua. Ali recovered instantly. It was as if he never had sore eyes.

Uthman b. Hunayf explains:

A blind man came to the noble Messenger and said:

– Oh Prophet of Allah, can you make a prayer to Allah so that I could see again?

– If you wish we can postpone this Dua until the Day of Judgment; this is better for you. But if you wish I could do it now, replied the noble Prophet.

The blind man said: "Pray for me now."

The noble Prophet then instructed him to perform Wudu and then two Raqats of Salah. He also taught him the prayer which he needed to recite. The blind man performed everything described by the Prophet and he regained his vision.

All creatures recognize the Messenger of Allah

During Hijrah, the Noble Prophet had taken refuge in a small cave along with Abu Bakr. A spider quickly spun its web to close the entrance of the cave. The idol worshippers had tracked down the Prophet and Abu Bakr all the way to the cave. Upon seeing the spider web at the entrance of the cave, they returned back assuming that the spider web would have been destroyed if they were there.

Jabir b. Abdullah explains:

– We were at a military expedition with the noble Messenger. Suddenly, my camel refused to move. The noble Messenger came next to me and touched the animal. My camel began to move so fast that I was pulling hard on the reins so that I could hear what the Prophet was saying.

Enes b. Malik explains:

A Jewish woman from Khaybar brought some meat to the noble Messenger. She had poisoned it. The noble Messenger ate the meat and nothing happened. Then the woman was brought to him. The noble Messenger asked her why she had poisoned the food. The woman answered:

– I wanted to kill you. The noble Messenger replied:

– Allah will not let you succeed.

According to Abu Dawud, the slaughtered lamb informed the Prophet that its leg had been poisoned.

Aisha explains:

We had a bird in our peaceful home. Each time the noble Messenger left the house, it began to fly around and move. The bird calmed down whenever the noble Prophet entered the house. When he was home the bird was calm and quite.

Enes b. Malik explains:

The noble Messenger was the most beautiful, the most generous and the most courageous of all human beings. One night the people of Medina were frightened by a noise they heard. A group of people walked carefully towards the sound, only to see that the noble Messenger was already there. He was riding bareback on Abu Talha's horse with a sword in his hand. The noble Messenger said:

— Do not be afraid! Abu Talha's horse is quite comfortable.

In fact, this horse had a reputation of being quite lazy. From that day on the horse became unbeatable in a race.

Rocks and mountains testify to the Messenger of Allah

Jabir explains:

— The noble Messenger once said: "I know a stone in Mecca that greeted me before I was given the mission of Prophethood. I still know it pretty well."

Abdullah Ibn Masud explains:

— When we ate with the noble Messenger, we could hear the food reciting the names of Allah.

Muslim transmits from Abu Hurayra:

— The noble Messenger, Abu Bakr, Umar, Uthman, Ali, Talha and Zubayr were standing on Mt Hira. The mountain began to tremor. The Messenger of Allah said, "Calm down Oh Hira, for there is a Prophet, a Siddiq and martyrs standing on top of you".

The Prophet was miraculously protected

According to Jabir's narration, he was with the Prophet on a military expedition to Najd. He also returned with the Prophet. On the way back, they had stopped in a valley that had plenty of trees. The Prophet dismounted his horse in order to rest. Others in the convoy chose a spot amongst the trees. The noble Messenger hung his sword on the branch of the tree and sat underneath it. We had closed our eyes to get some rest when we heard the noble Messenger call. We quickly rushed towards him. There was a Bedouin Arab sitting next to him. The noble Messenger explained what occurred:

— This man came when I was asleep. He had drawn my sword. Then he shouted:

— Are you afraid of me now!

— No, I am not afraid of you, I replied.

— Then who can protect you from my attack now? He asked.

– Allah will protect me! I replied. Then the angel Gabriel smacked him across the chest. He dropped the sword and quickly I grabbed it. Then I asked him:

– Who will protect you from me now? He replied:

– No one!

Abu Hurayra explains:

Abu Jahl pointed to Sajdah and asked:

– Does Muhammad still rub his face on the ground?

– Yes, someone answered. Then he said:

– I swear by Lat and Uzza that if I see him doing that again, I will step on his neck. Or I shall bury his face into the earth. A short while later, the noble Messenger began to perform Salah at Kabah. Abu Jahl walked up to him with the intention of stepping on his neck. Suddenly, he began to run away from the noble Prophet whilst trying to protect his face. They asked him:

– What happened?

– An abyss of fire appeared between me and him. There were scary beings with wings standing between us.

The noble Prophet then said:

– Had he approached me any further, the angels would have amputated his organs one by one.

Aisha explains:

"Until the verse, „no *doubt, Allah will protect you from people'*, was revealed, the noble Messenger was protected by his Companions. Following the revelation of this verse, the noble Messenger said, "Oh believers, I am under the protection of my Lord now!"

Prophet's prayers answered

Enes b. Malik explains:

The noble Messenger was delivering a sermon on Friday when a man came up to him and said:

– Oh Messenger of Allah, it hasn't rained for a long time. Pray to Allah so that He sends rain.

The noble Messenger made Dua immediately. In no time, it began to rain. It rained so much that we hardly made it to our homes. The rain continued until the following Friday.

Enes continued:

The following Friday another man stood up and said:

– Oh noble Messenger, pray to Allah so that the rains are scattered away from us. The noble Messenger prayed once

Oh Almighty Allah.

Take the rains away from us and distribute it outside of Medina.

I swear by Almighty Allah, the clouds began to split and move away. It was raining all around the boundaries of Medina whilst the residents of the city remained dry.

Once, our Prophet made the following Dua:

"My Lord, Almighty Allah! Honor one of these two (Umar Ibn Khattab or Abu Jahl) individuals with Islam. Glorify Islam through the one you are pleased with."

The following morning, Umar Ibn Khattab came to the noble Messenger and embraced Islam.

Abdullah b. Abbas explains:

The Prophet walked into the bathroom. I had placed a bowl of water by the door so that he could perform Wudu. He asked:

– Who put the water here?

– It was me, Oh Messenger of Allah, I replied. Upon hearing this, he prayed for me:

– My Lord Allah, grant him the wisdom of religion.

It is clear as daylight that the noble Messenger's prayer was accepted. Ibn Abbas became a renowned scholar and he was invited by Umar into the committee of scholars at a very young age.

According to Musnad, the Messenger had made the following Dua:

"My Lord Allah, give him awareness about the soul of religion and grant him the knowledge of interpretation".

Enes b. Malik explains:

My mother brought me to the Messenger of Allah and said:

– Messenger of Allah. This is my son, little Enes. I brought him to you. He shall serve you. Pray to Allah for him.

The noble Messenger prayed:

– Oh Mighty Allah, increase his wealth and give him many children.

I swear by Almighty Allah, I became rich and the number of my children and grandchildren is more than a hundred.

Enes b. Malik explains:

One day the noble Messenger came to visit Ummu Haram. My auntie offered some food to him. After eating, the noble Messenger slept for a short while. Then when he woke up, he was smiling. Ummu Haram asked:

– Oh Messenger of Allah, what made you so joyful?

– In my dream, I saw people traveling over high seas, on ships like kings on a throne. With all their glory they were heading towards a sea battle. Ummu Haram said:

– Pray to Allah so that I become one of those warriors of the sea, Oh noble Messenger of Allah.

The noble Messenger prayed for Ummu Haram.

Enes says, during the time when Muawiya b. Abu Sufyan was the governor of Damascus he commanded a fleet of ships in a sea battle (Cyprus). Ummu Haram was on one of the ships. After landing on shore, she fell off her mount and became a martyr.

Angels and Jinns appeared before the Prophet and spoke to him

Abdullah Ibn Umar explains: My father Umar Ibn Khattab said:

– One day we were with the Prophet when a man with a pure white garment and dark black hair came next to us. There were no signs on him suggesting that he had been traveling. No one amongst us knew this person. He sat next to the Prophet and touched his knees to the Prophet's. Then he began to ask a series of questions to the noble Messenger, regarding Islam, Iman, Ihsan and the Day of Judgment. The Messenger of Allah answered every question one by one. Following the question and answer session, the man suddenly stood up and went. I waited quite awhile. Then the noble Messenger turned to me and said:

– Oh Umar, do you know who that person was?

– Only Allah and his Messenger know, I replied.

– That was Angel Gabriel. He came to teach you your religion, said the noble Messenger.

Saad b. Abi Waqqas explains:

On the day of Uhud, I saw two men standing on the right and the left side of the noble Messenger. They were both wearing white garments. They were fighting vigorously to protect the Prophet. I had never seen these two before the battle and never saw them again. (The two individuals mentioned here are Gabriel and Mikhail).

Muaz b. Rifa'a transmits from his father, Rifa'a b. Rifa'a:

– During the battle of Badr, Gabriel came to the Prophet and asked:

– How do you see those who participated in the battle of Badr? The noble Messenger replied:

– We regard them as the most virtuous of all Muslims. The Angel said:

– The Angels who participated in the battle of Badr are also regarded as the most virtuous amongst us angels.

Ahmed Ibn Hanbal transmits a Hadith in his Musned, narrated by Ibn Masud. In the Hadith titled, "Laylaful Jinn", it is recorded that the noble Messenger taught Qur'an to the Jinns.

Premonitions and miracles regarding the future

Aisha explains:

– One day there was a solar eclipse. The noble Messenger performed his Salat-ul Kusuf and then he said:

"No doubt that the moon and the sun are two of Allah's verses. When an eclipse occurs, perform two Raqats of Salah. I swear by Almighty Allah that when I perform Kusuf, I observe everything that has been pledged to me on earth. When you see me move forward during the prayer, I see myself close enough to grab a handful of grapes from Paradise. When you see me move backwards, I see hell and its inhabitants being annihilated."

Abdullah Ibn Abbas explains:

The noble Messenger stopped between two graves and said:

"Beware; most certainly, these two are being punished. They are punished for serious sins. One of them did not protect himself from urine and the other was a slanderer."

The trees testify to him

Jabir b. Abdullah Explains:

We were walking with the Messenger of Allah. We came down to a big valley. The noble Messenger went to relieve himself. I walked after him with a bowl of water. He looked around for a place to conceal himself. Then he noticed two trees at the corner of the valley. He walked up to one of them and grabbed one of its branches. Then he spoke to it:

– With the permission of Allah, obey me. Like a camel pulled by its master, the branch bowed in front of the noble Messenger. Then he grabbed a branch from the other tree and repeated the same words. It too obeyed the noble Messenger. Then the Messenger of Allah stood between them and said:

– Cover me, with the permission of Allah! Abruptly, the branches covered him.

Abdullah b. Umar narrates:

– The noble Prophet used to deliver his sermon leaning on a block of timber made from a date tree. When a Minber was built, the Messenger refrained from using this block of timber. Suddenly, the timber made a groaning sound. The noble Messenger walked up to it and stroked it with his noble hand. Only then it stopped groaning.

Abu Said Al Hudri explains:

– One day, following the Isha prayer, the Messenger of Allah gave a stick to Qatada b. Numan. He then said to him:

– This stick will form a light ten feet ahead of you and ten feet behind you. You will see a dark shadowy figure just before you enter your house. Do not wait for it to speak to you. Strike it on the head with this stick. Qatada did exactly as the Prophet ordered.

2. Why did the man who ate halva, have himself stoned?

There was a man called Husayn in Afyon. He was Meczup and was given the title of 'man who ate Halva'.

All day he'd wonder around the streets of Afyon. No one understood the words he spoke. However, there was a unique spiritual side to the man who ate Halva. This is why the community tried to make sense of every sentence he muttered. The man who ate Halva would spend his nights at various chemists. Afyon was a cold place and he needed a place to keep warm at nights.

This is how I got to meet him. Whenever I went to the chemist at night, Husayn was there. After awhile, we became good friends. He opened up to me like he never did to anyone.

Being a doctor, there were many occasions where I had to rush to the hospital for emergencies. He would see the concern on my face and say "Don't worry doctor your patient will be all right". On some occasions he'd say, "Do not waste your time, he is gone". He had never been wrong. These were things that he would not tell anyone. For some reason, he trusted my friendship and spoke openly.

One day I was going to visit a child patient of mine. I had spent a lot of effort for this patient and honestly believed that he would recover. That day, his father came running. The child had a high temperature. I grabbed a box of penicillin from the chemist. Those days penicillin was a new drug. As I stepped out of the chemist, Husayn looked at me and said, "You are wasting your time doctor, the child is gone". As I approached the house on a horse carriage, I could hear the screams. The child had already passed away, I was deeply saddened.

The man who ate Halva had an interesting side to him. During the day he was on the streets, children would chase him and cast stones at him. Children teased him by shouting, "Halva eater...Halva eater!" He would frequently get upset and begin to throw insults at the kids. This however, encouraged them further as they continued to harass him. So the title, 'the man who ate Halva', originated from there.

In time, I got to know him better and trusting our friendship, I said, "Husayn, couldn't you find another job? It must be hard being a Dervish and getting stoned all day". He replied, "This is a mystery for you to solve. There is nothing better than what I do. This is a beautiful thing." This was quite a riddle which I never solved, until after Husayn had passed away. Husayn was performing a Sunnah. When the noble Messenger went to Taif, the children of this town had cast stones at him. Husayn was feeling the pain that the noble Messenger had experienced as stones hit his body. So, according to Husayn this was a Sunnah of the Prophet.

The man who ate Halva was an extraordinary man of spirituality. He possessed an extreme level of love for the noble Prophet. Hence he believed that if the Prophet was stoned, so should I. He was quite a Dervish.

"Pray to Allah so that you have an ounce of love for the Prophet. It is his love that bestows life on nations. The universe came to existence for his love. The precious gem concealed in existence, manifested itself because of his love. The soul can only find peace and tranquility through his love. Loving him is a day without a night.

3. Servanthood

The purpose of Prophethood crosses paths with the purpose of creation of mankind. This crossing point is servanthood.

In the holy Qur'an, Almighty Allah states: *"I have created the Jinn and the mankind so that they may worship me"* (51/56). Allah clearly points to the reality of servanthood.

This means that the main reason for our creation is to recognize Allah and to serve Him in an appropriate manner. Eating, drinking, earning money, buying a house or a car should not be our priority in life. Obviously, they are necessities of life, but they are not the purpose of our existence. For this reason the Prophets were sent to us, so that they may guide us onto this mysterious path.

Allah has indicated to this fact in the following verse: *"Not an apostle did We send before thee without this inspiration sent by Us to him: that there is no god but I; therefore worship and serve Me"* (Qur'an, 21/25).

In another verse, Allah stated: "For *we assuredly sent amongst every People an apostle,* (with the Command), *"Serve Allah, and eschew Evil": of the People were some whom Allah guided, and some on whom error became inevitably (established). So travel through the earth, and see what was the end of those who denied* (the Truth)." Allah lucidly indicates to the reason of Prophethood. They were sent to humanity so that people refrain from the idols and turn towards Allah. The Prophets guide humanity to servanthood.

The uniqueness of the Messenger of Allah

The rank of the noble Prophet is quite different to the others. He was sent as a mercy upon all worlds. He had the mission of guiding not only the whole of humanity but also the Jinn, to the right path. Abdullah Ibn Masud explains an incident which he had witnessed:

– One day, the noble Messenger took me to a place in the desert. He drew a circle around me and asked me to remain within the circle until he came back. He walked some distance away from me. Suddenly I began to hear some disturbing noises. I was in great concern for the noble Messenger's wellbeing. However, he had ordered me to remain in the circle. Sometime later, the Messenger of Allah returned. I asked him about the horrible noises I had heard. He replied:

– A group of Jinn came to offer their pledge to me. Then a conflict erupted amongst them. Believers began to fight with the nonbelievers. This was the noise you heard. Also, I was informed of the time of my death.

With the last sentence the noble Messenger was indicating to the following:

I was sent with a mission to guide human beings and the Jinn to the path of Allah. Today, even the Jinns have accepted my invitation.

This means that I have no reason to remain on earth anymore. Perhaps, it is time for me to leave.

His thoughts were also giving us a message regarding the mystifying purpose of Prophethood. He had taught us a Dua which established how we should make our preference between this world and Ahirah:

"Oh Almighty Allah, grant me a blessed life. And when death is better for me, take my soul, Oh Lord".

4. The pride of humanity

Question: The pride of humanity', he was born as himself, lived as himself and died as himself; what does this mean?

Answer: I have mentioned the sentence many years ago and it is difficult to remember all the details. However, I will attempt to illuminate the issue as much as my spiritual state allows me to do so.

Necip Fazil stated, "It is because of him we exist'. Although, some critics oppose the authenticity of this Hadith, the Qudsi Hadith which states, "I would not have created the universe, if it wasn't for you", strengthens the argument. Indeed, Allah created the universe because of him. The universe is a book which explains Allah, and Muhammad is its translator. Without him, this great book of universe would have remained as a mystery to us. We would have lived in it without understanding why and how. We couldn't have found Allah through the universe hence the universe would have no meaning. Whereas, the Almighty Allah states in the holy Qur'an, *"I have created mankind and the Jinn so that they may worship me"*. According to interpretation of Ibn Abbas, "Allah created existence in order to be known". This means that, without the Prophet we would not have understood the meaning of existence and recognized Allah. In this regard, we could say that he was the reason of creation.

All Prophets before him mentioned his arrival in their own way. For example, one of the great scholars of Andalusia, Qadi Iyaz, stated in his Sifa-i Serif: "Adam referred to him as an intercessor, following his extradition from paradise. He pleaded to Allah, "Forgive me Oh

Lord, in Muhammad's honor". The Almighty Allah asked, "How do you know Muhammad?" Adam replied, "I have seen the inscription, 'La Ilaha Illallah, Muhammadun Rasulallah' on the gates of Paradise. Someone whose name is written next to your exalted name must be of great value to you.

Jesus also mentioned him. Even in the current copies of the Bible, he states, "There is a lot I can say to you, for you cannot comprehend. I must go now, so that the leader of the world, the Holy Spirit, the separator of right and wrong could arrive to explain the truth to you." (Yuhanna, Chapter 16/12).

Jesus mentioned him as Ahmad. It is a divine fate that his grandfather, named him Muhammad, so that those in the heavens and those on earth would glorify him. Great personalities such as Imam Rabbani insisted on the truth of Muhammad and truth of Ahmed. He possessed the truth of Ahmed even before he came to this world. And with his mission on earth, he represented the truth of Muhammad. The gem of all Prophets has attained the truth of Muhammad by physical means, as a result of his representation. And again by achieving the truth of Muhammad, he has returned to being the soul of existence with the title of Ahmed.

Many mysterious occurrences took place on the night of his birth. According to Siyer, all the idols in Kabah had fallen; the columns in the palace of Persia had collapsed; the great fire of the Persian fire-worshippers, which had been lit for a thousand years, had been extinguished.

He was always protected by Allah, even as a child. For example, during his youth, he was helping in the renovations of Kabah. He was carrying stones when his uncle, Ibn Abbas suggested that he should place his garment under the stone to prevent a shoulder injury. As he lifted his garment, his legs became visible. He fell unconscious as soon as someone had indicated to it. Following his recovery, he was never seen in such a situation again.

The ignorant Arabs of that era were merciless tyrants. They were afraid of poverty so much that some buried their young girls alive. They were ashamed of having female children. Interestingly, they also possessed some virtuous manners. For example, generosity and courage were two important elements of their lives. We observed that all of their poetry contained these two themes. They had powerful literature skills. This is why Umar offered to recite a few passages from Ibn Ebi Salt at various gatherings. Also, trustworthiness was very important to them. They would protect everything that was entrusted upon them. In this regard, the noble Prophet was a way ahead of all of them. So much so that everyone gave him the title of 'Muhammad the trustworthy'. In addition, he had left all literature and poetry behind him, because he had received the holy Qur'an. This was so obvious that if all the poets of Arabia came together, they could not even write a single passage that resembled a verse from the Qur'an. Most certainly, he was a miracle of literature, words of wisdom and methodology.

At a time when he was harassed and insulted, Allah honored him with Miraj. Even the Archangel Gabriel could only accompany him to a certain level. He had to stop at some point and say, "Oh Muhammad! I cannot escort you any further. From this point on, everything belongs to you."

In the colorful words of Nizami, "For him, stars became stepping stones; angels became his servants, the crescent moon was like a horseshoe under his mount and the sun took refuge under the source of his luminosity."

We shall continue with a simple analogy to enlighten the issue: Everyone who passes by the great Mosque of Selimiye will experience a different feeling. For example, an expert architect will feel a sense of gratification upon observing its magnificent art. A shepherd will feel something within his own degree of understanding. Another example is that everyone's sense of taste is different. There are expert food critics who will detect flavors that normal individuals cannot. Just as the example, he experienced and sensed everything in a different way. In appearance, he was just like us but he lived in a different dimension. There were times that when he stood up to perform Salah, Janna (paradise) suddenly appeared before him. He would sometimes take a step towards it. Sometimes, he would take a step back upon the manifestation of something else. Through Miraj, he had reached the limits of humanity. That was the beginning point of eternity. He was not a God, nor could he ever be one. For this reason, the holy Qur'an referred to him as a man who had reached a point between absolute and possibility (Between Allah and creation).

Hadith critics have different views regarding his experience at Miraj. However, all Sufis believe that he had stepped out of the boundaries of space-time and beheld Allah in exoneration. Even after reaching such a level, he had chosen to return to earth hence he did. He only came back for his Ummah. Abdul Kuddus who was a great scholar, once said, "If I had reached such a level and was given the option, I would have never returned to earth again." Yet, the Prophet had returned to the people who harassed and insulted him, only with the purpose of guiding them and others like us, into the Paradise we had lost. At the very least, he made us aware of this feeling. As Mawlana Rumi explained, "he lived his life amongst people but with Allah. Whilst he had one foot in the seventy two nationalities of the world, the other was secured in truth."

The Prophet was extremely modest. Once, a woman saw him sitting on the ground to have some food. She said, "You are eating on the ground, like a slave". The noble Messenger replied, "Can you find a better slave than me? I am the slave of Allah".

Above all, he was a servant. There was a mention of starvation once, when Angel Gabriel was sitting beside him. The angel asked him if he preferred to be an emperor or a simple servant. He chose to be a servant messenger of God.

He was modest on the day he began his mission and modest on the day he entered Mecca on his camel as a victorious leader. He had bowed his head down, so much so that his forehead almost touched the saddle of his camel. Yes...he curved in modesty before Allah. A western thinker once said, "He continued his symphony of Prophethood with the same tune he had commenced and concluded on the highest note."

In conclusion, the Prophet was born as himself, lived as himself and when he had completed his mission, he died as himself. There were no other limits for him to reach or barriers to breach so he departed from this world as himself. He was so modest that during his illness he'd ask for Dua from Aisha. In his last days, Aisha had taken his hand into her own and decided to ask for a Dua, because the Prophet was so ill. The noble Messenger quickly removed his hand from Aisha's palm and raised it high. Then he made the following Dua,

"Allah is the greatest friend". Yes, he had completed his spiritual journey through the earth.

Let us complete our words with Mehmet Akif Ersoy:

"Whatever the world has, it was all because of him. The society is indebted to him and so each member of it. The whole of humanity is indebted to this innocent soul. Oh Lord, resurrect us with this testimony on the day of Judgment.

CHAPTER TWELVE

1. The sunnah of the Prophet

Whoever observes my Sunnah during the time of conflict will receive the reward of a hundred martyrs. (Hadith) Even the smallest acts performed with the intention of Sunnah will be transformed into a rewarding worship.

"Say (Oh Muhammad); follow my path if you love Allah, so that Allah loves you" (verse). Obviously, those who believe Allah will obey his command... The most acceptable and the shortest route to obedience is following the path shown by the individual whom Allah loves the most.

The Sunnah of the Prophet is same as virtuous behavior. "My Lord has given me the best of all manners and ethics." (Hadith) Whoever abandons my Sunnah has also abandoned good manners. Hence those who abandon good manners will be deprived of the mercy of Allah.

It is a great possibility that those who abandon Sunnah will go astray and fail into Bid'at.

The act of Sunnah contains a light that is so powerful that when compared, all Nafile is like a firefly next to sunlight.

2. Seven thousand pieces of gold

During the time of Hekimoglu Ali Pasha, there was a poor man who loved Allah. He had been in poverty for so long that one day he raised his hands and made a Dua:

– Oh Lord, you know my situation. I have run out of patience. My children are suffering. I cannot repay my debts. For the sake of your Messenger, show me a way out.

Following his sincere supplication he went to bed. A few hours later he began to see a dream full of mysteries.

The noble Prophet was standing before a poor Muslim and giving him the following advice:

– You have shown so much patience for so many years and passed the test of poverty. Allah heard your prayer and accepted your plea. Your problems are over. After performing the Morning Prayer, go to Hekimoglu Ali Pasha and give him my Selam. Tell him to give you a thousand pieces of gold. If he doesn't believe you, tell him that you went to sleep without reciting the Salavat you recite every Friday night. This will be enough to convince him.

The next morning, he went to Ali Pasha and explained his dream. There was no response from Ali Pasha. Suddenly, he said: "Explain your dream to me again". Once again the poor man explained his dream in detail. Ali Pasha paused for a brief moment and said: "Explain it again". Ali Pasha had asked the man to explain his dream seven times in a row. The poor man had lost hope and in disappointment he said:

– My dear Pasha, if you do not believe me and if you think that my dream has no value, just let me know. Do not make me repeat myself over and over. Ali Pasha was deeply affected by the reply.

– God forbid...God forbid! What do you mean I do not believe you? How can you say that I find your dream worthless? On the contrary, this is the most beautiful thing that has ever happened to me. It is so valuable to me that I did not want to rush through it with a thousand pieces of gold. Each time you explained your dream, in which the noble Messenger sends his Selam to me, I had allocated a thousand gold pieces for you. I wanted you to repeat it over and over again so that I could reward you again and again. So far, you have explained your dream seven times in a row so I shall give you seven thousand pieces of gold.

Ali Pasha then summoned his servant and ordered that seven thousand gold coins be paid to this poor man.

This poor man who loved the noble Messenger so much had been expecting a thousand gold coins from Ali Pasha. Yet, he was rewarded with seven thousand. From that day on, he lived a happy life with his family and children.

3. Respecting Prophet's heritage

It is difficult to say I love them. According to my worn-out mentality and broken heart, I believe that I love them. This is like a breeze that comes and goes. We feel that we sincerely love Abu Bakr and Umar... I feel that if Umar requested my soul, I would lovingly give it to him. I may be wrong.. .perhaps I am not quite sincere about this. Oh Lord, we believe that we truly love them all. If this is not true, please make it true. And if we truly love them, resurrect us with them and by their side.

Umar was a Caliph. They say that he was the Caliph of Allah and His noble Messenger. Umar represented Allah on earth with his names and attributes. He played a role in forming an initiative that belonged to Allah. He was a Caliph and delivered sermons. The spirit of the noble messenger had affected his soul so much that when he spoke, he interpreted all things that originated from the noble messenger. He represented the noble messenger so much so that the scholar of the Ummah, Ibn Abbas, rushed to the places wherever Umar spoke. If Umar was in Mecca, Ibn Abbas would go to Mecca; if Umar was in Medina, Ibn Abbas came to Medina. Let us now go back and observe an episode from Umar's life:

Here he is on his way to deliver a sermon. His mind is preoccupied with the preparation when a few drops of blood cause a stain on his garment. The blood had leaked from a drainage located on top of a house he was passing by. Umar returns home and changes his clothes.

He then rushes back to the Masjid and on his way he stops by the same house and rips the drainage pipe off the wall. Then he walks up the Minber to deliver his Khutba. After completing his Khutba, Umar takes one step down and cautions the Jamaat. "Brothers, do not cause problems for the believers. I was on my way to the prayer. As I passed by the wall of a certain house, a few drops of blood ruined my garment. I had to go back and change my clothes. So, on my way back to the Masjid, I pulled that drainage pipe down." Suddenly, everyone turns towards another direction. They are all looking at a person standing up in the Jamaat. It is quite obvious that this man's heart is broken. He is a man whom Umar loves so much. Many times he had prayed for rain with this person. Each time he raised his hands and said, "Oh Lord, these are the hands of the Prophet's uncle, send us rain for his sake."

The person who had stood up was Ibn Abbas. His face had turned pale as he walked slowly towards Umar. With great disappointment on his face, he asked, "What have you done Oh Umar? That was my terrace. I was there, on the day that the Messenger of Allah placed that drainage pipe with his own hands!" Umar had lost his balance even before Ibn Abbas could complete his words. In shock, he tumbled down from the Minber. Umar was on the floor of the Masjid. Suddenly, the following words begin to flow out of Umar's mouth: "Oh Abbas...I have a pledge to you. We will go to your house and I will place my head on the ground. You will then step on my face and attach the drainage pipe back into its place."

The Jamaat was in shock. Perhaps the number of people standing outside the Masjid was more than double. They were not aware of what took place inside the Masjid. The Caliph stepped out of the Masjid and walked through the Jamaat. He rushed over to the house of Ibn Abbas to fulfill his pledge. May your rank be Jannat al Firdaws, O great Umar. You are Umar. The man who caused the demise of the great Roman Empire. You are Umar, the man who brought down the great Persian Empire. Umar, the man who extinguished the fire of the fire-worshippers... Umar, who took the bangles of the Sasanid ruler and placed them in Suraka's arm. Then he went down to Sajdah, as he shouted "this was foretold by the Prophet!"

With all his awe and gallantry, Umar kneeled down next to the wall of Ibn Abbas. Ibn Abbas was refusing to step on his head. How could he step on a head that led all the Muslims? This was a noble head constantly preoccupied with strategies of defeating the enemies of Allah. Yes, it was a head that possessed a mind that thought of nothing but the pleasure of Allah. Do it, Oh Abbas! I deserve it! This is the head of a man who destroyed a pipe that was placed by the Messenger of Allah!

This was the mentality of the Companions. This was their way of respecting the noble Prophet's heritage. How about you, young man? Do the holy Qur'an and its generation have less value than an old drainage pipe in your mind? Why do you refuse to place your head on the ground? Will you not place your bow down as they attempt to tear the Messenger of Allah from your heart? Yes...you did not weep; at least you should have been ashamed to laugh. They stepped all over your land and you did not even weep. You should have at least shed a few tears during the night. You should have felt pain as they removed the noble Messenger from your society to replace him with Maoism, Marxism and Leninism! The noble Messenger had not entered your heart as much as a drainage pipe! May Allah forgive me and you!

4. Astonishing formulas proposed by the Prophet

Astonishing formulas that show humanity the path to peace and happiness proposed by an illiterate man following his visit to a cave clearly proves that these are not his doings. Before he entered the cave, everyone including friends and the enemy knew that he could not write or read. He had never even touched the Torah or the Bible. However, when he came out of the cave, he brought something that would take his people and all of humanity to eternal happiness. It would make role models of his people, which humanity would take examples of until the Day of Judgment, considering that the society he lived in was so barbaric that they took pride in burying their young girls alive. They had dived into an ocean of alcohol where you could not differentiate if it was blood or alcohol that flowed through their veins. He would interact with these people and take them up to levels that even the stars would envy.

They could not call him a liar because then they would have had to admit that they were deceived for forty years. Yet this was impossible, because a person could not change his ways after living forty years of his life in honesty and trust. Let us explain this with an example:

Think about a shepherd that makes a fool out of an entire society for forty years by deceiving them into believing that he was a doctor. Let us assume that he could trick a few people into believing him. How about an entire community or millions of people for hundreds of years? Is this possible?

Think about a person who is a compulsive liar. Could he lie to an entire society, including his relatives and friends and convince them that he is the most truthful person in the world? Could he trick everyone throughout his entire life? Obviously, this is impossible.

Even his enemies did not deny his acts. They tried to explain his acts by associating them to magic. This is another proof of his miracles. They had all seen the splitting of the moon and claimed that it was magic.

They had never refuted what he had brought. The noble Messenger challenged them with verses from the Qur'an: "Let them bring a verse resembling a short verse from the Qur'an. Let them call upon all the assistance they need". They had no answer to the Prophet's challenge of logic so they resorted to violence. This is one of the firmest evidences to his Prophethood. Why would anyone risk their lives against an opponent that could be silenced with a few words? The people of that era were quite talented in literature and poetry. One sentence from a poet triggered wars and another sentence established peace. These were the people who had achieved great development in literature. They should have easily prepared materials to challenge the Prophet but they were helpless against the Qur'an, hence they resorted to violence and put their lives and wealth under threat.

The virtuous character of the Prophet was recognized even by the enemy: The idol worshippers were forbidding people from reciting the Qur'an. Some of the chieftains such as Abu Jahl, Abu Sufyan and Ahnes Ibn Shurayk, desperately kept people away from the Qur'an whilst they themselves secretly listened to its recitation. What attracted people towards the Qur'an? A man who did not even know how to read or write was explaining something to the people and those who visited him were changing their lives so much that they would sacrifice their lives lovingly for what they had learned. They would never betray their cause no matter what sort of torture and torment they faced. The nonbelievers wondered about the driving force that gave them this dedication.

The answers to these kinds of questions brought them together around the Prophet's house almost every night. They were listening to the holy Qur'an recited by the noble Messenger, until sunrise. At first they were not aware of each other's presence. When they found out, they began to blame each other and promised never to return again. Perhaps, they did not want to go there but the curiosity had overwhelmed them. The following night they were all there again.

When they saw each other, they all became angry. They said, "We try to keep people away from him yet we come here to listen. If people were to find out, we will fall into a difficult situation. From now on we should never come here again". So they gave their words and went home. However, they were there again the next night. This time they made a strong pledge and kept it.

What they had heard were not the words of a madman. These chieftains were the political and economical leaders of the people hence they possessed more knowledge than the average member of the community. For this reason, they knew that the words spoken by the Prophet were not nonsense or mere poetry. They also knew that unless they did something about this, it was going to be too late. However, something prevented them from going to him. It was their ego, stubbornness and personal interests. Indeed, they knew the truth but their pride prevented them from following a poor orphan. They were saying, (God forbid) "How could Allah choose a poor orphan when there are wealthy nobles like us?"

It is a common thing that when we come up with a simple idea that will be beneficial to people, we do not hold back. We feel like mentioning it to everyone. At gatherings, when there is a topic that we are familiar with, we choose to speak. Especially when the issue concerns life or death, we would feel that it is imperative to say what we know. If we keep quite in such situations and as a result something terrible happens, we would feel guilty and question ourselves, "Why didn't I say something?" Or others may say, "If you knew something that could have prevented this disaster, then why didn't you speak?" Those who keep quite against tyranny and suffering will be judged by the conscience of society. This is a good example for those who live in a society that has serious problems, and do not speak even though they have knowledge.

Following the analogy, let us take a good look at the situation of the Prophet. For humanity, the knowledge he possessed was necessary as bread and water. His knowledge was a light that would brighten the even the darkness which lied beyond the grave. The truth he proposed would save a barbaric community that buried their girls alive and bring them up to a level that even the stars in the sky would envy. These were the values that humanity had waited for so long like a dehydrated person in the middle of the desert. If the noble Prophet knew all these precious remedies before the age of forty and kept it to himself, wouldn't society and his own conscience judge him?

This psychological analysis clearly proves that he did not possess this knowledge before the age of forty. Most certainly, he would have spoken had he knew. Otherwise, his conscience would have bothered him. Then we must admit the fact that Allah gave him the knowledge and he passed it over to us.

Success did not change him: The fact that the noble Messenger showed no sign of a change in his behavior and lifestyle even after tremendous success and fascinating accomplishments is the greatest evidence of his Prophethood. Indeed, he continued to be a modest person and chose a life of poverty over wealth. He was an amazing person of Taqwa and Zuhd. Let us leave his Taqwa for another time and take a look at his Zuhd.

Zuhd: This is a state of mind that if the world was given to him he would not display joy and if he had lost everything in the world, he would not be distraught. When he began his mission, he was sitting on a simple mat and when he climbed to the highest peaks, he continued to sleep on a mat made up of straws. One day, Umar had seen him sleeping on his modest mat and felt so emotional that he began to weep. The noble Prophet asked what made him so touchy. Umar replied:

– Oh Messenger of Allah, leaders in your position sleep in beds made up of bird feathers, but you sleep on a piece of mat made up of straws. How could this be when the universe was created because of you?"

– O Umar, would you not prefer paradise over this world?

One night, he could not get an ounce of sleep. He tossed and turned making sounds of concern. His dear wife asked the following morning: "Oh Messenger of Allah, you seemed distressed and troubled throughout the night. Are you feeling ill?" The noble Messenger replied: "Before I went to sleep, I found a date on the floor and ate it. Then I realized that we had some dates of Zakat and Sadaqa at home. What if the date I ate was one of them? In agony, I thought about it until the morning". Zakat and Sadaqa was Haram for him. The date he ate could have been one of the gifts that were brought to him, but even the uncertainty made him distressed. At this point we should stop and think. If this person was not a Prophet who believed that he would be held accountable for everything he did on earth, why would he go through all this trouble?

Evidently, there is a place where everyone would be questioned about their actions. Yes. . .with this feeling, the noble Messenger lived a very sensitive life. He became a role model to others and continues to do so. The way he was when he had nothing, did not change when everything came under his command. He was the same man when he began his mission and the same man when he had completed it.

Even when the world began to smile at him, his attitude towards the world did not change. He was like a fasting man on earth who waited the time of Ahirah so that he could break his fast. When Angel Azrail gave him the choice of keeping his soul or passing it over to him, he chose to go beyond, next to the greatest companion.

Face also testifies to one's honesty: Sometimes, the human face is a great indication of a person's honesty or dishonesty. Some scholars and experts are able to figure out whether a person is lying or not by the signs on their face. This is science and in the Arabic language, it is called "The knowledge of Kiyafet". It is a knowledge that establishes a person's character by studying his face, hands and feet. Under the guidance of this knowledge, the great Jewish Scholar Abdullah Ibn Selam looked at the Prophet's face and stated, "There is no lie in this face!" His conclusion was also based on indications stated in both the Torah and the Bible. He was so sure of the Prophet that he made the following historical statement: "I may have doubts about my wife, even about my children but I could never doubt the fact that the great Prophet described in the Torah and the Bible is no other than Muhammad (peace and blessings be upon him)". The value of gold is best understood by a goldsmith. If we are failing to understand him, this does not mean that the essence of the noble Prophet is not gold but it means that we are not goldsmiths.

In politics, politicians frequently use their opponent's past against them:

If the noble Prophet was not speaking the truth and making up some of the things he said (God forgive us for the description), then he would have blundered or made a gaffe in his life time of 63 years. Therefore, his enemies who were looking for an opportunity to refute the Prophet would have found his mistakes and used them against him. Take a good look at the political leaders of today. They would use every opportunity to pull their opponents down. It is a common thing for them to use their opponent's past against them. Those who have broken the law in the past either pull out of the candidacy race or risk their political careers by continuing. No one gets away with anything. Developed nations with advanced systems do not even forgive the smallest errors made by their politicians. The institute of politics is at the bottom of the ocean compared to the institute of Prophethood, which is at the top of a mountain. If faults are detected so easily at the bottom of the ocean, then imagine the conditions on top of the mountain. The noble Prophet was on top of a platform that required great sensitivity. There were opponents who would resort to anything for their cause. They were all looking for the smallest error on behalf of the Prophet yet they found nothing. If they had found something, this would have benefited them more than anyone. Since there was no logical or rational way of defeating the Prophet, they resorted to violence and chose a path that placed their lives in danger. This was a clear proof that they could never defeat the Prophet in knowledge and wisdom.

An imitation of something will never be the same as the original. Can anyone deceive you by presenting a candle light and claiming that it is sunlight? Scientists cannot be tricked into believing that a fly is a peacock, candlelight is the sun or a shepherd is a governor or an academic. Just as the example, it is impossible to trick people into believing that a man was a Prophet for 23 years.

It is quite difficult for a person to come up with a series of lies in a small community and in addition to this, practice the lies he told, to the smallest detail. Especially, in a mission such as Prophethood where people believed him so much that they were ready to sacrifice their lives for him.

How can anyone assume that a man with no education could deceive and trick an entire community, especially when there were many men of wisdom amongst them?

The greatest evidence to the authenticity of his mission was that he risked his life for his cause even though he was all alone for a long period of time. Throughout his ordeal and struggle, you will not find even a moment of hesitation.

He emerged with an important mission but what was more important is that he practiced what he had preached. He encouraged people to pray, fast and give alms and he performed these deeds more than anyone.

Another proof is that all the unique attributes and beauty possessed by the previous Prophets were incorporated in his noble person. If all the essential characteristics of Prophets were at their highest degree in him, then we have no other alternative but to call him a Prophet. How could a person who never lied to human beings, lie to Allah?

5. Sending salatu salaam to the noble Prophet

Will Allah bring down mercy and peace upon his Prophet because of our Salatu Salaam? The mercy of Allah is already upon the noble Messenger. Then what is the divine reason for our Salatu Salaam?

The Messenger of Allah is like a nucleus at the foundation of all virtue and blessings. He is a guide who shows humanity the right path, indicates to Sirat al Mustaqiym and a leader who cannot be deceived and will not deceive. He is a complete role model.

That individual who guides everyone onto this path of Nur will receive his share of the rewards collected by all believers. According to the principle, "cause is like the doer", the noble Prophet will receive a share out of all good deeds performed by his Ummah. This means that if you are the cause of a deed – good or bad – you will receive your share of the reward or punishment.

The noble Prophet is the possessor of 'Makami Mahmud', hence his book of rewards do not close upon his death. Rewards in abundance will continue to be recorded in his book. Therefore, his rank will continue to increase and his authority will extend. There are two ways of approaching the issue:

Firstly, by sending Salatu Salaam to the noble Messenger, we are renewing our pledge to be his Ummah. In another words, we are saying, "we remember and think of you. We pray to Allah so that He may increase your rank." Looking at the issue from this perspective, since we are pleading to Allah for the noble Prophet, we become eligible for his intercession (Sefaat) hence his circle of intercession grows. This in turn gives more and more people the opportunity to benefit from his intercession.

Secondly, making Dua for the noble Prophet means that the person making the Dua receives the benefits of going under the protection of the noble Messenger. So, with the inclusion of this person, the circle of intercession becomes larger. Therefore, in actual fact we are in need of the Salatu Salaam more than the Prophet. By sending Salatu Salaam, we are declaring his greatness and our weakness at the same time. Like a person seeking refuge in his nation, we are seeking refuge in the noble Prophet, in realization of our weakness and in fear of the great Day of Judgment.

May Allah grant us all, the intercession of Allah's Messenger, the owner of Sefaat-i Uzma.

Let us not forget to mention the signs indicating to this fact. The noble Prophet stated: "All Prophets have given something to their Ummah. I have reserved my right and saved it for Ahirah. This is the right to be an intercessor to my Ummah".

6. Taking example of the Prophet's manner

A man, who did not take the Prophet's manner as an example, saw the Prophet one night in his dream. The noble Messenger did not even take any notice of him. The man asked, "Have I done something to disappoint you, O noble Messenger?"

The noble Prophet replied, "No".

Once again, the man asked, "then why do you turn away from me?"

"I do not know you" the noble Messenger replied. The man was surprised as he said, "How could this be possible? I am one of your Ummah and the scholars taught us that you could identify a member of your Ummah even better than their own mother".

The noble Messenger replied: "This is true. However, I do not observe any of my manners on you and you have never sent a Salatu Salaam to me. I can only identify my Ummah if they bear signs of my manners".

When the man woke up in the morning, he pondered on what he had seen. Then he decided to practice the good manners of the noble Prophet. Sometime later, the noble Prophet came into his dream again and said:

"I recognize you now and I will make intercession for you. The reason for this was that the man truly loved the Prophet now, because he decided to emulate his manners.

7. Those who love are those who know

The rank of believers by the side of Allah and the noble Prophet can be measured by the love they show towards them. Whoever loves Allah and his Messenger the most, will be the closest to them. The approval of Allah is proportional to proximity. One will live in the hope of his compassion, mercy and clemency, depending on his proximity to Allah. Therefore, those that distance themselves from Him will be deprived of His compassion, mercy and sympathy.

Blessings and favors of Allah are also proportional to His approval. Those who have achieved His approval have also earned His compassion, mercy and blessings. As a result, Allah becomes their seeing eye, functioning hand and a close friend in all situations. It is imperative that every believer makes this a principle of priority for themselves. They should evaluate the blessings and favors of Allah with the love and passion they possess in their hearts. They should also try to attain a sincere love for Allah, so that they could seek for the approval of Allah. Allah's approval means receiving His aid. Those who do not feel the waves of rejoice attracted by His love, are far apart from the mercy and approval of Allah. In order to close this gap, they must sincerely seek for the companionship of Allah's blessing and favor. This can only be achieved by displaying serious effort on His path.

Perfection can only be achieved by recognizing His divine Names and attributes, and by understanding Muhammad, who is the best reflector of these luminous divine attributes. This is the only condition and necessity of being a perfect human. Otherwise, we will resemble those liars who claim to perform miracles so that they could be respected as wise individuals.

In reply to the blessings, favors and mercy of Allah, we should also display benevolence. Our benevolence towards Allah should be in the form of worship, as if we were seeing Him and following His Messenger by holding tightly onto his robe. If Allah is bestowing blessings upon us, this means that He wants us to show gratitude by thanking Him with our body, mind, heart and soul. We must thank Him by following the noble Messenger in total submission. Great disappointment and regret awaits those who refuse to follow His Messenger. Those who do not show their gratitude will eventually run out of energy hence never reach their goals in life.

Our primary duty is to study and recognize Muhammad, learn the Qur'an at an expert level and possess detailed knowledge about Allah and His divine names. This is the only way through which we can attain true love for them.

Those who love are those who know. Indeed, those who truly love and recognize Allah say, "When will I return to you, O Lord?" And those who love his Prophet say, "When will I reunite with you, O noble Messenger?"

Fatima was born after the noble Messenger received his mission of Prophethood. She was raised with special care and courtesy. The generation of the noble Prophet was to continue through Hasan and Husayn. This golden generation of Nur which would brighten the whole of humanity began with Fatima.

When the Surah Nasr was revealed, although Fatima was only in her twenties, this intelligent woman sensed that it was almost time for the Prophet to leave. She cried passionately. Of course, there was nothing she could do hence the Prophet died. However, just prior to his death, she brought her ear next to his mouth. As the noble Prophet said a few words to her, she began to cry. Then he continued with a few more words, this time she began to smile with joy.

Aisha, who had witnessed the whole incident asked, "What did he say to you?" Fatima replied, "First he said that he would not recover from this illness. This made me cry. Then the second time, he said that I would be the first person from his family to join him, and this made me happy. Yes, I felt blissful because I would also leave this world soon to join Allah and His Messenger".

A believer's love and recognition of the Prophet can be measured by his/her infatuation to join him. Those who do not love him do not know him. After knowing him, one cannot abstain from loving him. Yes, when you love the Prophet, a handful of soil from his homeland becomes more precious than the entire world. You become obsessed with him, crying each time you hear his noble name.

Abu Bakr as Siddiq explains:

– One day we were sitting with him. The time of Asr had passed and the sun was about to set over the mountain. The noble Messenger began to speak and what I heard was like the end of the world to me. He said, "Allah gave His servant a choice to stay here or go beyond. His servant chose the latter…" I could not hold back my emotions, hence I wept loudly. The servant he mentioned was himself. Allah had said to him, "If you wish I will collect your soul now." I said to the noble Messenger, "Allow us to sacrifice ourselves, mothers, fathers and families for you, but you remain here. Let us all die for you, but you stay".

Ibn Masud explains:

– The noble Messenger summoned us to the house of Aisha. It was a week before his death. There was no sign of an illness. He lifted his head and looked at my face. Then he wept. Leaving his loyal friends made him emotional. Perhaps, he would not see many of them until the day they all entered Paradise. He spoke a few words in the state of an emotional atmosphere. "Salaam to you all. May Allah be your aid. May the clemency of Allah remain upon you. Stay within the boundaries of your testimony. You have defended His religion. May Allah protect you until the Day of Judgment." The noble Messenger made these prayers and then continued with tears in his eyes, "The world of Ahirah is a place for those who abstained from arrogance and pride in this world. It is for those who constantly focused on the life after." Then he recited the following verse, *"Innehu meyyitun wa innehum meyyitun"*. For those who did not understand, he continued with the following words, "Death is near. It is time to return to Allah. It is time to turn towards 'Sidratul Munteha'. Then he wept again. By this time we realized what he meant and all of us began to weep. We did not know how long he had but frequently we would come together and weep because of his imminent departure. During his illness, he would come to us with a bandage over his head. He tried to calm us down. No one had stopped crying. Then we asked him, "Who will wash you, Oh noble Messenger?" He indicated to Ali. "Who will place you in the grave, Oh noble Messenger?" He replied to his family, "Place my body near the grave, and then stand at a distance, because my Salah will be performed by Gabriel, Mikhail, Israfil and Azrail first. You will perform Salah following the Angels.

The Companions were devastated. Their days had transformed into night and their nights became as dark as a grave. They were deeply distressed by the noble Messenger's departure. Even at a time like this, they were showing great sensitivity towards the orders of the noble Prophet and performing their duties to the smallest detail.

May Allah control our disobedient carnal souls and rebellious Satans who refuse to recognize him. Muhammad, peace and blessings be upon him, is a soul that even the trees, mountains, stones and worlds admired and obeyed. May Allah command our carnal souls and Satans to embrace him also. May Allah protect us from going astray. May He allow us to continue on His straight path in devotion and dedication. Amin.

8. Observing the Prophet's sunnah in our daily lives

1) Using our right (hand or foot) in virtuous acts and using our left in certain regular tasks.
2) Washing our hands before and after food consumption.
3) Beginning with Bismillah prior to eating, contemplating on the blessings of Allah during dining and declaring our gratitude at the end by saying, 'Shukur'.
4) During dinner, eating from our own side of the plate.
5) Eating on the floor. If necessary, a table may be used.
6) Commencing to eat at the same time with others on the table.
7) Abstaining from eating when we do not feel hungry. Getting up from the table before our stomach is full.
8) Serving a small amount in the plate and not leaving leftovers.
9) When eating on the floor, leaving the right knee raised and bending the left knee.
10) It is Haram for Muslim men to wear gold and silk accessories.
11) Spreading the Salaam around. Remembering that Salaam comes before words.
12) When entering the house, giving Salaam first to the household.
13) Smiling and embracing one another with a sincere Salaam.
14) A sincere hug may be allowed with the handshake.
15) When shaking hands it is ethical not to pull your hand away before the other person.
16) Kissing the hands of religious leaders, scholars and government leaders is permitted. Giving Salaam to old ladies and

kissing their hand is allowed when necessary. As long as there is no possibility of Fitna.

17) Exchanging gifts is good behavior. When we receive a gift, it is nice to reply with a similar or a better one.
18) Abstaining from laughing a lot. It is better to smile than to laugh.
19) Keeping silent most of the time and speaking only when necessary.
20) Speaking clearly in a medium tone and repeating important issues three times.
21) Beginning with the name of Allah and concluding with His name.
22) Controlling anger. It is important not to get upset over worldly issues and matters concerning our carnal soul. One should only display anger over issues of defending Allah and His religion.
23) Even jokes should be based on truth.
24) Refraining from useless activities.
25) When going to bed, we should lie down on our right side and place our head within our right palm. And we must think about what we have done during the day.
26) Abstaining from sleeping face down.
27) Before going to sleep, bringing your hands together in an open position and reciting, Ikhlas, Falaq and Nas. Then blowing into your hands and rubbing the entire body three times.
28) Wearing white.
29) Using Mest.
30) Putting your shoes on, beginning with the right foot, taking them off beginning with the left.
31) Covering your head with a cap or Turban during Salah.
32) One should not go to the Masjid or gatherings after consuming onion or Garlic.
33) Abstaining from entering the toilet or places alike with materials that contain verses or Surah from the holy Qur'an.

34) Being hospitable to visitors and guests by offering food, etc., to them. Greeting the guests with clean, tidy clothes.
35) Following a sneeze, saying *'Alhamdulillah'* with a firm voice. In reply, others should say, *'Yarhamukallah'*. The person who sneezed then should reply with, *'Yahdina wa Yahdikumullah'*. This may be repeated three times. If a person sneezes more than three times in a row, then it is not necessary, because this is a sign of flu.
36) Concealing a yawn as much as possible. It is good to close the mouth with the hand. During a prayer, if one needs to yawn, covering the mouth with the right hand in a standing position is recommended. In all other positions, it is better to use the back of the left hand.
37) Attending invitations and accepting gifts.
38) We should not knock on someone's door more than three times. If the door does not open, we should turn back and walk away. When the person in the house asks, "Who is it?" We should not reply, "It is me". We must identify ourselves in a proper manner. We should not stand right in front of the door to take a peek inside the house. It is good manners to stand by the side of the door.
39) Refraining from urinating in a standing position. Protecting our clothes from urine spill. In a Hadith it is stated that most of the punishment in the grave will be because of urine spillage. Making sure that when sitting on the toilet we are not facing Kabah or our back is not turned towards it.
40) We should never urinate in the bathroom.
41) Refraining from urinating in public places such as parks and roads. Also, abstaining from spitting and making a mess in public places. In a Hadith, the noble Prophet fears that those who act this way may be condemned.
42) Taking great care with bodily cleanness. Shaving the underarms and other private parts. This must not be done during

the period of being Junup. Washing up before the shave is recommended.

43) When entering public baths or saunas we must take great care with our covering.

44) It is good to use Miswaq or a brush to clean our teeth each time we perform Wudu. According to some scholars, Miswaq is used with the intention of cleaning our teeth, getting rid of mouth odor, killing the bacteria and keeping our mouth healthy. Therefore, a brush that does the same job as a Miswaq may be used.

45) Consultation with pious and trustable people and then following the decision made.

46) Being generous. "Generosity brings one closer to Allah and stinginess takes one away from Allah." Generosity is a tree in paradise with a branch hanging down into this world. Whoever, grabs this branch, it will take him to Janna.

47) One must frequently contemplate, think and ponder. Meditation and contemplation will get rid of indolence. Pondering about death will transform the temporary pleasures into bitter tastes. Deep thoughts will manifest the seal of mortality which exists on all matter.

48) When borrowing money or other things, we must prepare a documentation clearly displaying the agreement. This is not being distrustful. This is done to prevent misinterpretations in the future. The entire agreement should be clear and comprehensible.

49) Offering condolences to a Muslim whose relative has passed away. The prayer should be in the following format, "May Allah grant mercy upon him/her". The visit for condolences should be made within the three days. It is inappropriate to remind the household of their loss after three days, because it would refresh their sorrow. Close relatives of the deceased may not be able to prepare food for a few days, so caring neighbors should prepare food for them.

This will show that they are sharing their sorrow. Close relatives of the deceased should make themselves available for at least three days, so that believers could visit and offer their condolences.

50) Remembering the dead in a blessed manner.
51) One should not mourn the dead in a rebellious manner, such as screaming out loud, hitting oneself or pulling one's own hair. This type of behavior is an indication of rebellion against the will of Allah. It is a form of revolt against destiny. Behaving in such manner will not help the deceased.
52) Encouraging those who are about to die by asking them to repeat the words, "La Ilaha Illallah Muhammadun Rasulallah". Using a clean, wet towel to keep the person's lips moist. Recitation should be ceased upon the person's death. We can continue to recite Surah from the holy Qur'an at a certain distance away from the body. The dead person's chin should be kept closed using a handkerchief or a similar material. If the person has died with their eyes open, they should be closed.
53) Visiting the cemetery will abolish indolence and cause one to contemplate on life after death. As we approach the entrance of the cemetery, we should greet the people of the Kabir with the following words, "Assalamu Alaykum ya Ahlal Kubr, you came here before us. We shall follow you. We wish for the mercy and forgiveness of Allah upon you". We should then approach the grave of the deceased we intend to visit from the direction of his/her feet. It is appropriate to stand facing towards Kabah. We may recite verses from the Qur'an and make Dua. It is Makruh to step on graves. If there is no other way of passing through, then we should walk through by offering a Hasene to the deceased in the grave. The grass or weeds on top of the graves should not be pulled out; on the contrary we should plant flowers. Dead or dried out weeds may be removed.
54) Visiting ill relatives, friends and companions. Giving them morale and hope. Keeping visits short. Abstaining from talking

about the condition of the ill person at other places. (If this is going to displease the ill person)

55) Keeping in touch with relatives and family members. "The mercy of Allah will not come down on a gathering in which there is a person who has cut ties with his relatives."

56) Drinking Zam Zam water in a standing position and facing Kabah in respect.

57) Displaying obedience to your mother and father. Caring for them and looking after them. Abstaining from breaking their hearts and receiving their blessings and Dua.